Doing Business Successfully in China

T0348594

CHANDOS
ASIAN STUDIES SERIES:
CONTEMPORARY ISSUES AND TRENDS

Series Editor: Professor Chris Rowley,
Centre for Research on Asian Management, Cass Business School,
City University, UK; HEAD Foundation, Singapore
(email: c.rowley@city.ac.uk)

Chandos Publishing is pleased to publish this major Series of books entitled *Asian Studies: Contemporary Issues and Trends*. The Series Editor is Professor Chris Rowley, Director, Centre for Research on Asian Management, City University, UK and Director, Research and Publications, HEAD Foundation, Singapore.

Asia has clearly undergone some major transformations in recent years and books in the Series examine this transformation from a number of perspectives: economic, management, social, political and cultural. We seek authors from a broad range of areas and disciplinary interests: covering, for example, business/management, political science, social science, history, sociology, gender studies, ethnography, economics and international relations, etc.

Importantly, the Series examines both current developments and possible future trends. The Series is aimed at an international market of academics and professionals working in the area. The books have been specially commissioned from leading authors. The objective is to provide the reader with an authoritative view of current thinking.

New authors: we would be delighted to hear from you if you have an idea for a book. We are interested in both shorter, practically orientated publications (45,000+ words) and longer, theoretical monographs (75,000–100,000 words). Our books can be single, joint or multi author volumes. If you have an idea for a book, please contact the publishers or Professor Chris Rowley, the Series Editor.

Dr Glyn Jones
Chandos Publishing
Email: gjones@chandospublishing.com
www.chandospublishing.com

Professor Chris Rowley
Cass Business School, City University
Email: c.rowley@city.ac.uk
www.cass.city.ac.uk/faculty/c.rowley

Chandos Publishing: Chandos Publishing is an imprint of Woodhead Publishing Limited. The aim of Chandos Publishing is to publish books of the highest possible standard: books that are both intellectually stimulating and innovative.

We are delighted and proud to count our authors from such well known international organisations as the Asian Institute of Technology, Tsinghua University, Kookmin University, Kobe University, Kyoto Sangyo University, London School of Economics, University of Oxford, Michigan State University, Getty Research Library, University of Texas at Austin, University of South Australia, University of Newcastle, Australia, University of Melbourne, ILO, Max-Planck Institute, Duke University and the leading law firm Clifford Chance.

A key feature of Chandos Publishing's activities is the service it offers its authors and customers. Chandos Publishing recognises that its authors are at the core of its publishing ethos, and authors are treated in a friendly, efficient and timely manner. Chandos Publishing's books are marketed on an international basis, via its range of overseas agents and representatives.

Professor Chris Rowley: Dr Rowley, BA, MA (Warwick), DPhil (Nuffield College, Oxford) is Subject Group leader and the inaugural Professor of Human Resource Management at Cass Business School, City University, London, UK, and Director of Research and Publications for the HEAD Foundation, Singapore. He is the founding Director of the multi-disciplinary and internationally networked Centre for Research on Asian Management (http://www.cass.city.ac.uk/cram/index.html) and Editor of the leading journal *Asia Pacific Business Review* (www.tandf.co.uk/journals/titles/13602381.asp). He is well known and highly regarded in the area, with visiting appointments at leading Asian universities and top journal Editorial Boards in the UK, Asia and the US. He has given a range of talks and lectures to universities, companies and organisations internationally with research and consultancy experience with unions, business and government, and his previous employment includes varied work in both the public and private sectors. Professor Rowley researches in a range of areas, including international and comparative human resource management and Asia Pacific management and business. He has been awarded grants from the British Academy, an ESRC AIM International Study Fellowship and gained a 5-year RCUK Fellowship in Asian Business and Management. He acts as a reviewer for many funding bodies, as well as for numerous journals and publishers. Professor Rowley publishes extensively, including in leading US and UK journals, with over 370 articles, books, chapters and other contributions.

Bulk orders: some organizations buy a number of copies of our books. If you are interested in doing this, we would be pleased to discuss a discount. Please email info@chandospublishing.com or telephone +44 (0) 1993 848726.

Doing Business Successfully in China

MONA CHUNG

CHANDOS
PUBLISHING

Oxford Cambridge Philadelphia New Delhi

Chandos Publishing
Hexagon House
Avenue 4
Station Lane
Witney
Oxford OX28 4BN
UK
Tel: +44 (0) 1993 848726
Email: info@chandospublishing.com
www.chandospublishing.com

Chandos Publishing is an imprint of Woodhead Publishing Limited

Woodhead Publishing Limited
80 High Street
Sawston
Cambridge CB22 3HJ
UK
Tel: +44 (0) 1223 499140
Fax: +44 (0) 1223 832819
www.woodheadpublishing.com

First published in 2011

ISBN:
978-1-84334-548-0 (Chandos Publishing)

978 0 85709 155 0 (Woodhead Publishing)

© M. Chung, 2011

British Library Cataloguing-in-Publication Data.
A catalogue record for this book is available from the British Library.

Typeset by RefineCatch Limited, Bungay, Suffolk

Contents

List of figures

About the author

Dr Mona Chung is a bicultural expert in cross-cultural negotiations whose work addresses the cultural gaps between Westerners and Chinese in the fields of commerce and education. Not understanding or ignoring the vast cultural differences between Australia and China has contributed to many companies suffering heavy financial losses over many years.

Dr Chung has extensive experience in Western–Chinese business relationships. She specialises in strategic planning, management and marketing practices on behalf of international organisations (commercial and educational). As a bicultural person, she short-circuits processes and produces results that increase efficiency by between 70 per cent and 50 per cent with significant cost savings.

Dr Chung is on the executive board of the Victoria branch of the Australia China Business Council. Being highly experienced in a large number of industries and a frequent visitor to China, Dr Chung is a guest speaker at many public forums and author of an extensive list of publications in cross-cultural business studies. This is her second book on how to do business in China. Her first, in 2008, was *Shanghaied: Why Foster's Could Not Survive China.*

Dr Chung lectures at Deakin University, Australia and can be contacted on +61 414271678 or info@ccinternational. net.au.

Introduction

Abstract: Chapter one gives an overview of the book and emphasis on the importance of bicultural negotiators. It starts with high lighting the importance of doing business with China today especially in the relationship with US. It states that doing business with China today is a 'must' for all organisations. Therefore organisations must pay attention to the fundamental determining factor-cultural differences. This book focuses on this point and draws full attention to the key issue in doing business with China – to understand its culture and do business the Chinese way in China to ensure success – hence doing business successfully in China.

Key words: China, doing business in China, doing business with Chinese, Chinese economy, Chinese market, cultural differences, The Glass Wall Effect, bicultural negotiators.

The importance of doing business with China

In 2010, as people in the world's long-established and emerging economics pondered whether they had finally survived the global financial crisis, or were heading towards another, even deeper recession, the position of China continued to change rapidly on the international stage in many ways. Foremost in this regard is economic development, closely followed by political positioning. The world's number one economy, the United States, is now being seriously challenged by China.

Attached to this challenge is an increasing tension between the US and China on a number of issues: trade, currency valuation and debt level. On the surface they are economically related matters, but history tells us that economics is closely linked to political influence. The US–China political relationship has not been so tense since the visit by US President Richard Nixon to Beijing in 1972. It is clearly an arm wrestle between the US and China for the title of number one economic power and this means future political dominance. For Western nations, at least, political clout coupled with economic strength has always meant trade dominance.

Against this background, it is essential to understand the importance of China internationally. To all Western organisations and businesses, China is no longer a choice but a necessity for their future. Doing business with China is now a 'must', and they must get it right.

This introduces the question of how to do business successfully in China. Businesses large and small began testing the waters with business activities in China as soon as its open-door policy was tentatively implemented in 1979. Since then, for more than 30 years, and specifically in the first 20, a large number of companies have lost thousands of billions of dollars between them in this most attractive market.

China's economic importance as a market and the dominating position of its manufacturing capacity has made it a very attractive destination for international businesses. China's current position as the manufacturing base of the world means that organisations find it difficult to avoid direct or indirect involvement. Yet after all this time, and the now obvious urgent need to understand how the Chinese do business and how 'outsiders' must conduct business with them, there is no commonly available publication on 'doing business with China' that combines a theoretical framework with knowledge gained from practical experience.

The core emphasis of this book is on how cultural differences affect companies' return on investment. The book aims to provide executives and entrepreneurs with a golden opportunity to succeed in the Chinese market, instead of suffering the fate of many others in the past. As one business executive has said: 'the path to the Chinese market is littered with corpses'.

The lure of 1.3 billion consumers

Multinational companies around the world entered the Chinese market for a simple reason: its 1.3 billion consumers. From a purely strategic viewpoint this has proven to be unsuccessful, simply because of the cultural complexity of China's vast mass of potential customers. Without culturally suited marketing strategies, billions of dollars were poured into China and it became a giant black hole for many marketers. This book looks at why it is essential when marketing products to the Chinese to take cultural differences into consideration. It draws on research by the author into the Foster's Group experience of three joint ventures with Chinese breweries from 1993 to 2006. (This research, for a PhD project, led to her first book: *Shanghaied: Why Foster's Could Not Survive China.*)

All marketing activities, anywhere, begin with an analysis of the market and a process of formulating strategies and plans, according to all trained marketers and their text books. Some argue that setting up the right strategies is crucial to success in international business; others believe the implementation of strategy is more important. It is argued here that establishing correct strategies is a prerequisite for adequate implementation.

Being a huge market of rapidly growing prosperity and social change, China is attractive to multinational corporations around the world. In 2006 it was the second-largest recipient of foreign direct investment in the world, according to US statistics. Companies from around the world have been pursuing the Chinese market in a more focused manner since China's economic reforms in the late 1970s. Inward investment in China in 2005 and 2006 was approximately $70 billion a year. However, only a very small number of firms are meeting profitability projections and many others have made large capital writedowns. Most US and European multinational corporations have never made a profit in China.

Communication is fundamental to all business activities, and cross-cultural communication is far more complex than mono-cultural communication. The problems of communicating with multiple stakeholders embedded in diverse cultures are complex. These are exacerbated by the linking of macro-cultural issues, such as globalisation, with micro-cultural and community identity issues. In relation to doing business in China, communication has been the most important issue that has caused tremendous difficulties. For this reason, communication with Chinese is best conducted by those with a depth of knowledge and skills.

Different behavioural patterns may cause inefficiency in a cross-cultural communication process. Misunderstanding across different cultures is harder to recognise than in mono-cultural communication and is more difficult to deal with. Cultural capability is caused by an inability, or varying degrees of ability, to interpret cross-cultural behaviour. Not understanding culturally related behaviour often results in a complete misunderstanding when encoding and decoding messages. Communication is, in effect, blocked not by one barrier but by too many barriers.

A little knowledge can be dangerous

With increasing business activities in China, more and more people are benefiting from the experience of visiting, working or studying in China. But many of them are in danger of suffering from the Glass Wall Effect (discussed further in chapter 2).

In some cases prior knowledge or experience of a culture is misleading and unhelpful in dealing with cross-cultural situations. People may be caught in a situation where they cannot explain differences in behaviour. For example, knowledge in dealing with Japanese may give false confidence in dealing with Chinese, by thinking that 'Asian' cultures are all the same, or similar. This is especially confusing when Asians of Chinese background present themselves as Chinese – an ethnic group, rather than a nationality group.

The importance of competent and trained interpreters cannot be emphasised enough, because half-baked cultural knowledge, and incompetent language skills in both English and Chinese, are likely to confuse matters rather than clarify them.

Differences in the expertise of individual interpreters engaged by Westerners and Chinese are unavoidable and therefore an imbalance in the spoken communication processes is likely to occur and miscommunication is equally inevitable.

By understanding this, Western companies will also understand the importance of engaging good interpreters who have competent cultural knowledge of Australia and China, as well as competent English and Chinese language skills.

Current and constant change

This book is timely as while it is in production China's position is changing on a daily basis.

The increasingly important and controversial position of China in world trade raises the topic of negotiating with the Chinese on a new level of importance. In more recent years, this topic has become increasingly interesting from both sides of the negotiations. Although Chinese universities and publications pay much more attention to the topic than do Western universities and literature, the actual business activities suggest that both Chinese and Westerners have equally poor negotiation results.

Bicultural negotiators are the most effective. They are familiar with both cultures, are capable of effective communication beyond language skills in both cultures, and can switch between each at ease. This is the key to successful negotiation with the Chinese.

Negotiations with Chinese are never concluded. When a contract is signed and an agreement is reached, it is not the end of the negotiation. It is really just the start of an understanding. Issues that have been negotiated or not negotiated may surface at any time before or after signing. Anything is subject to negotiation and renegotiation. Contracts symbolise the beginning of a long-term cooperative relationship rather than steps and details to be followed. When contracts are signed, few details are usually included. This is not a matter of respecting or not respecting a piece of paper; rather, it is recognised that circumstances change constantly and flexibility is essential.

The Chinese culture is a collective one. They do everything in plurals, including one job being performed by more than one person. In the Chinese language, there is no plural form of nouns; numbers are added to particular nouns. At times, deliberate vagueness can be tolerated. Chinese teams do not make major decisions on the spot or allow decisions to be made by individuals. This is most obvious when a negotiation team is small, regardless of its members' rank and power.

As well as the fundamentals of doing business in China, the following chapters pay specific attention to negotiations with the Chinese. More importantly, this book gives theoretical and practical advice on doing business with China and doing it successfully.

2

Communicating with Chinese by understanding them better

Abstract: This chapter starts with basics in communication then moves on to the cross-cultural communication, in specific communication with China. It introduces the concept of high-low context culture and language and communication styles. With real case examples it demonstrates how relationships are built in doing business with Chinese.

A main point of this chapter is on the Glass Wall Effect, explains what it is and why it is more dangerous than no knowledge at all. It goes on to explain the pros and cons of using an interpreter and how miscommunication may occur. Suggestions are given to Western companies to ensure that they have their own interpreters when negotiating with Chinese.

Key words: communication with Chinese, communication model, high and low context culture and language, relationship building with Chinese, communication styles, miscommunication across cultures, the Glass Wall Effect, and explains the role of interpreters in cross-cultural communication.

The increasing use of globalisation as a strategy for growth leaves organisations no choice but to ensure they have effective cross-cultural communication skills and processes in place. Communication is fundamental to all business activities, and cross-cultural communication is far more complex than mono-cultural communication. The problems of communicating with multiple stakeholders embedded in diverse cultures are complex. This is exacerbated by the linking of macro-cultural issues, such as globalisation, with micro-cultural and community identity issues.

Communication models

To help understand communication, let us look at some basic communication models. The model used by Shannon and Weaver (Dwyer 2002, p. 53) has been the most popular so far in improving communication in organisations (see Fig. 2.1).

Its main elements (sender, receiver, encoding, decoding, channel, message and context) explain factors behind ineffective communication. Factors such as culture, technology, environment, individual differences and others may affect these basic elements, which indicate the complexity of any effective communication process.

Within one culture, barriers to communication occur at any point. For instance, individuality determines how a sender may encode a message. Within one cultural community, Foster's Group head office in Melbourne for example, certain protocols exist for how a message should be sent. When a

Figure 2.1   The Shannon–Weaver Mathematical Model, 1949

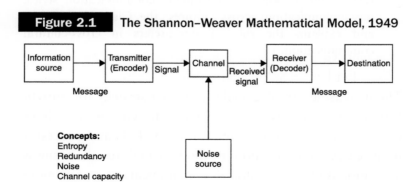

sender behaves abnormally (as perceived by others and they are usually from the same cultural group), the receiver will have difficulty in decoding the message. This may cause suspicion or distrust, or possibly even a conspiracy theory, in processes of communication. Further misunderstanding may occur through the feedback loop, which in most cases is how a misunderstanding is discovered. When a misunderstanding is not recognised by either the sender or receiver, behaviour framed by the misunderstanding will influence the new pattern of communication. This will cause further misunderstandings and, in turn, damage relationships.

In communication with Chinese, this process is often the main cause of misunderstanding, because culturally Chinese are less likely to clarify issues for two reasons:

1. Their communication style – high context compared with low context.

2. The culture of being vague as well as polite, 'hanxu (含蓄)' is considered a good quality in a person.

Different behavioural patterns may cause inefficiency in a cross-cultural communication process. Misunderstanding across different cultures is harder to recognise than in mono-cultural communication and is more difficult to deal with. Cultural capability is caused by an inability, or varying degrees of ability, to interpret cross-cultural behaviour. Not understanding culturally related behaviour often results in a complete misunderstanding when encoding and decoding messages. Communication is, in effect, blocked not by one barrier but by too many barriers.

Increasing diversity worldwide has drawn much attention to cultural issues in communication. Previous literature suggests that in communication across cultures, context is the component that causes most difficulties. Cultural differences substantially affect the process of message transmission.

Context of culture and cross-cultural communication

Edward Hall's theory of high context and low context culture is fundamental to the understanding of cross-cultural communication and styles. Hall (1976) suggested that on a continuum of a scale, people of different cultures can be divided into high and low context.

Context is the information that surrounds an event; it is inextricably bound up with the meaning of that event. The elements that combine to produce a given meaning – events and context – are in different proportions depending on the culture. The cultures of the world can be compared on a scale from high to low context (Hall and Hall 1990).

High and low context is a continuum scale that indicates the degree to which someone is aware of the selective screen that they place between themselves and the outside world. I find this concept is one of the most useful in explaining the differences between individuals, and at the same time, the concept is broad and covers such large groups and numbers of people.

On a macro level, the concept is brilliant and even on a micro level I have used it to explain many situations, and people are generally enlightened by it. However, for every example one can possibly find an exception.

People of high context culture communicate with high context messages in a high context manner, and vice versa in low context culture. In high context, the unspoken meaning is at least as important as what is actually said, while in low context culture most of the information is expressed explicitly. In high context culture, people express themselves with many and a large variety of words. They go around the issues and expect the listener to understand the hidden agenda. The speaker expects the listener to follow their train of thought and to pick up the meaning between the words. Surrounding context and background information are part of what is expected to be familiar to all. Among people of the same culture, this is achieved without the need for clarification.

For instance, in negotiations, Chinese often use the expression, 'the price is too high' as a smokescreen. This can have several meanings, such as: the price is genuinely too high and the other party needs to bring it down; or there is a hidden agenda because the real issue is not price, but they cannot express the real issue concisely.

It is expected that the other party, if also from a high context culture, will pick this up and quickly work out exactly what the real issue is. However, not understanding the cultural background makes it difficult, if not impossible, to decode the real meaning. The importance of this concept of high and low context is clearly seen in miscommunication between cultures or alternatively the ease with which people of the same cultural group communicate.

Communication in a high context culture takes much longer to reach the point of exchange (Korac-Kakabadse et al. 2001) and it contains attempts to smooth over any unpleasant information that has to be conveyed (Hall and Hall 1990). It has been said that the difference between Americans (low context) and Japanese (high context) is: 'When we say one word, we understand 10, but here (in Japan) you say 10 to understand one' (Kennedy and Everest 1996). People of low context culture are so economical in using words. They put meaning to each word and only express the exact meaning of the words they use. For people of high context culture, meanings cannot be expressed directly; to do so is simply rude.

This difference between the two cultures has a big effect on the effectiveness of their communication. Culture is the primary force of human behaviour and hence communication style. The differences, or the inability to interpret correct meanings from people of one culture to another, are the main barrier to effective cross-cultural communication. Using language as the only excuse is shallow. Language difficulties are merely symptoms rather than the cause.

Building relationships at all levels

Culture as a whole can be likened to an onion. There are many layers to the concept of culture, hence the cause of difficulty may appear at many different levels, which often causes confusion in a cross-cultural context.

Communication in a high context culture usually involves multiple levels of relationships in different situations. For instance, when Chinese receive Western visitors in China, the visitors will be looked after for the duration of their stay. From morning to night, programs and activities are organised from the minute they arrive to when they board the plane to depart. The hosts will extend hospitality to accompanying family and friends or at least say, 'Next time, bring your family.'

Chinese ensure that all visitors are well looked after and entertained as a part of relationship building and it is considered good manners and appropriate hospitality. To keep visitors accompanied 'peizhe (陪着)' is basic manners for hosts and hostesses. Often when facilities permit, visitors' accommodation costs are usually also covered. Difficulties occur when Chinese visit Australia. Unenlightened Westerners expect them to get from airport to hotel by themselves, and entertain themselves when there are no business-related activities.

Not only is the reciprocal level of hospitality poor in Chinese eyes, but they are often at a loss to understand why. Serious consequences have occurred from these types of inhospitable arrangements and sadly few lessons have been learned, as an example from a few years ago shows.

A Chinese mining company visited Melbourne to negotiate a contract with BHP Billiton. The meeting was held promptly on time at BHP's office. At its 12.30 pm conclusion, the Chinese were politely shown the way out. Standing in the street with little idea where they were, they phoned a Chinese friend who one of the delegation members knew. The conversation ensued:

> 'We just had our meeting with BHP.'
> 'How did that go?'
> 'Well, and we just finished now.'
> 'Good, are they taking you to lunch?'
> 'Not really, as a matter of fact we are just standing here at (location), wondering where we should go for lunch. Are you free for lunch?'

At lunch, the Chinese delegation disclosed the purpose of their trip and when asked how the negotiations went, they said: 'We need to buy this much of (product). Do you want the contract?'

BHP negotiators would not have found out about this mistake because they would simply have assumed the Chinese were insincere and did not get back to them.

On another occasion one of the many higher education institutions in Melbourne with a large number of Asian students told some visitors from a Chinese university to 'grab a cab and come to (destination)' when they phoned from the airport. They did and arrived for the scheduled meeting. Afterwards they were left to stop another cab themselves, on a freeway at 1 pm. The Chinese delegates waited 45 minutes before a cab would stop. Needless to say, they never returned to the Australian university.

The Australian university simply commented later: 'Chinese universities often come and visit, but never come back.' No one even asked the question, if a delegation (usually more than four people) bother to spend tens of thousands of dollars visiting Australia, why would they not wish to produce an outcome?

Questions and answers not always straightforward

Low context culture people discuss very specific topics. They ask specific questions, straight to the point, and expect direct answers. They are seldom able to read behind the words of the answer to look for hidden agendas, or interpret words differently from how they are presented.

On the continuum of high context and low contexts, Chinese are placed on the most extreme end of high context, and Westerners are pretty much at the other end of the scale. This gives us some inkling of the likelihood of effectiveness when Chinese communicate with Westerners.

With this in mind, miscommunication can easily occur. The large gap culturally between Westerners and Chinese may result in the communication going in the totally opposite direction to what was intended.

For instance, when Chinese negotiate in their wordy manner and do not express explicit meanings, Australians will be drawing conclusions from the words presented rather than looking for the hidden agendas and the meanings between the words. In the meantime, the Chinese will not believe that explicit words mean what they seem to mean but will be guessing the 'real' meanings. This will further increase the misunderstanding and heighten miscommunication.

Another difference between high context and low context cultures in communication style is that high context people (Chinese) express their ideas implicitly, using lots of implicit supporting evidence. Often, on the surface, this evidence does not appear to be directly related to the main topic. Chinese communicate using the popular approach of combining several philosophies and systems of logic (which can be culturally biased) throughout an explanation to demonstrate certain points. This may totally confuse Westerners who have the opposite style and logic.

Westerners communicate by stating results explicitly from the beginning and supporting them with evidence. This cultural group is seen as direct, sometimes blunt, especially by Chinese. Low context Westerners express their opinions and ideas without hesitation, expecting the receiver to reply and express their opinions through the feedback loop in the same manner. Ideas, opinions, suggestions and decisions may be refined through a series of communication processes.

This fundamental difference in approach makes communication between high context and low context cultures very difficult unless briefing and/or training is provided beforehand.

Context becomes even more important in understanding messages that have the potential to be distorted or omitted altogether. These distortions and omissions can only be noticed by people of a different culture in a communication process. This is because of the different cultural context. Listeners within the same culture are already 'contextualised', so do not need to be given much concrete background information. On the other hand, listeners from a different culture will need to be 'contextualised' first. This can be a lengthy process.

Understanding high context and low context culture also helps in understanding how people relate to each other, especially through social bonds, responsibility, commitment, social harmony and communication (Kim, Pan, and Park 1998). People of high context culture tend to be deeply involved with each other; in low context culture, people are highly individualised, somewhat alienated and fragmented, and there is relatively little involvement with others (Hall 1976). Chinese, who are collective and high context cultural people, behave in the most connected and relationship orientated manner, which is the very opposite to Westerners, who are low context individualists.

The communication pattern of people from a low context culture providing a high level of content and a low level of words, and high context people providing a high level of words but a low level of content, is the major reason that Chinese often regard Westerners as 'silly', because they give direct and precise information, leaving no room for guessing games. For people from a high context culture, it is not nearly complex enough.

As for the results of negotiations, high context negotiators gather more information during talks than low context negotiators. This serves as an astute strategy for high context negotiators to prepare for the later stages of the negotiation (Chung 2008).

A tough negotiation I was involved in relating to the Australian Retirement Living Group (ARLG) is a good example of how a mixture of high context and low context culture works in negotiation. The first visit the group made to China was to negotiate the possibility of collaboration or investments with a Chinese investment group in Changzhou. It was going to be tough because we knew the only competitor was a large US company with more than 300 retirement homes and investments in 50 countries. ARLG was a combination of an architecture firm, a retirement living group and a consultant from China.

Limitations in practical situations

There are limitations in applying the context concept to all cultures. First, to simply divide all cultures into high and low context means that at each spectrum a very wide range of different cultures is covered, which creates inaccuracy (Hall 1976). Second, in determining at which end of the spectrum a culture belongs, personal bias has a strong influence (Kim, Pan, and Park 1998). In other words, the determination of one individual by another of their position on the scale from high to low context is highly dependent upon the culture of the person making the judgement.

If that person is from a culture on the extreme end of the low context scale, they are likely to judge a high context person as being on the further end of the high context scale than the actual position on the scale; a low context person who is more towards the middle of the scale is likely to put the same person at the lower end of high context.

The measuring process is far too fluid to reach any definite conclusions. This eliminates accuracy in cross-cultural studies at the macro level. However, the question is posed as to whether one is ever able to determine the exact position on the scale of culture, because the concept is such a complex topic. Nevertheless, the concept of high context and low context culture provides the basis of understanding people of different cultures, and of not taking a situation for granted.

Miscommunication across cultures

The essence of communication is the exchange of information, with information being the carrier of meaning. Between different cultures, the perception of those sending the message may be totally different to the perception of their audience (Condon and Yousef 2002; Chaney and Martin 2004; Tian and Emery 2002). Therefore, identifying the audience and designing the message according to the perception of the audience, instead of that of the sender, before transmitting it, is a sound way of ensuring effective communication.

The complexity of communication processes determines that miscommunication always involves communication across cultures (Coupland, Wiemann, and Giles 1991). Cross-cultural communication relies deeply on the designing, transmitting and receiving of messages.

Understanding cultural differences is the basis of effective cross-cultural communication. 'When communicators come from different backgrounds, the potential for misunderstandings is greater. Culture provides a perceptual filter that influences the way we interpret even the simplest event' (Adler and Rodman 2000). Therefore for a cross-cultural communication process to be effective, the ability to translate the cultural context (Chung 2008) rather than just the words is essential.

Although knowledge and the study of cultural differences can reduce the 'noise' in communication processes and improve the effectiveness (Tse et al. 1988), without the successful translation of cultural context, miscommunication is inevitable. It is this requirement for successful translation at the cultural level that often cannot be achieved.

As mentioned, cultural differences determine the ways people behave, and hence communicate. In a Chinese–Westerner negotiation process, two groups often start by testing the communication methodologies until a mutually understood pattern is established. Where differences are greater between the parties, this pattern may never be established.

This process is fertile ground for misunderstandings, which are generally minor at the beginning. The real danger is when miscommunication is caused by cultural differences that neither party is aware of. In many cases the miscommunication continues without being detected until a major communication breakdown occurs. This is common in Western–Chinese negotiations because when Chinese are not clear about a message they are unlikely to initiate discussions to clarify the matter. The normal action for Chinese is to walk away for fear of causing conflict.

The Glass Wall Effect

The Glass Wall Effect relates to when people observe the behaviour of people of a foreign culture as if from the other side of a glass wall. They do not realise the barrier exists because they cannot see it. The barrier consists of prior knowledge or experience of the foreign culture that has created bias in understanding (Chung 2008).

The Glass Wall Effect as a concept addresses questions that were fundamental to my early research for this book. Does prior knowledge of, and training in, a culture create a situation where parties are under the false impression that all cross-cultural behaviour is understood, yet in reality it is found to be difficult to comprehend? Does such a phenomenon become an invisible barrier to cross-cultural communication?

In some cases prior knowledge or experience of a culture is misleading and unhelpful in dealing with cross-cultural situations. People may be caught in a situation where they cannot explain differences in behaviour. For example, knowledge in dealing with Japanese may give false confidence in dealing with Chinese, thinking that 'Asian' cultures are all the same, or similar. This is especially confusing when Asians of Chinese background present themselves as Chinese – an ethnic group, rather than a nationality group.

People who observe cross-cultural behaviour from the other side of the glass are the primary victims of the Glass Wall Effect. When they are placed in another new culture, their prior knowledge and experience of a previous different culture leads them to make little or no effort to adjust.

This concept may be extended to a false Glass Wall Effect; that is, when certain behaviour is the norm in one culture it is assumed the same behaviour is also the norm in another. For instance, in Japan, to appreciate tasty noodles, it is acceptable to slurp. Mistakenly, people with Japanese experience do the same in China, especially if they are exposed to very cheap street eating. In reality, slurping noodles is simply a sign of bad manners in Chinese culture, but it is often done by a large number of Chinese.

This is because until recently, 80 per cent of the Chinese population grew up in the countryside and had little education. A smaller percentage (50 to 60 per cent) of the population now lives in the countryside but a majority are still not tertiary educated. Further, Chinese mannerisms tend to be taught through family education rather than schooling. The false Glass Wall Effect can therefore be a bigger danger culturally because it is hidden and, without deep cultural awareness, will not be realised.

Foster's Brewing expatriates with experience working at Foster's Fiji before going to China in the 1990s repeatedly suggested that China was 'easy' when they first arrived. But it was soon recognised that China was very different to Fiji and many of them described the Chinese culture as 'alien'. Their Fiji experience might have helped to create a Glass Wall Effect.

The Glass Wall Effect may also be seen in people working in a foreign culture who have had short-term cross-cultural training, say two weeks before departure, giving a false sense of security. A typical example: After a one-day training course I conducted, one participant commented, 'Now I have learnt so much and I know doing business with Chinese is all just about trust and relationships.' He quickly organised a trip to China to visit some business contacts. In all future negotiation sessions he would start by saying, 'I know doing business in China is all based on trust and relationships . . .' He was soon telling others that he knew all about doing business with Chinese, which was about trust and relationships, nothing else.

The Glass Wall Effect in practice – a deadly sin

With increasing business activities in China, more and more people are getting experience in visiting, working or studying in China. Many of these people are in danger of suffering from the Glass Wall Effect.

I was in a delegation where one member had spent about a year in China in the past. The problems were that he had spent most of his time with expats; and having a Westerner's perspective, he thought he knew about China, whereas learning everything about China (if that is possible) would have taken many years of living, thinking and acting as a Chinese. He was unable to read the language and could speak only a few words, and could not pick up the non-verbals at a critical negotiation session.

Fortunately it was not a disaster because I was closely involved in the negotiation and interpretation. The negotiation session was tough as I was representing a small Australian company with one shareholder. I knew the competitor that had been negotiating with the Chinese company was a large established US firm with 20 years' experience in the particular industry, and more than 300 facilities and investments in over 50 countries.

Strictly speaking, the Australian company was not even in a position to compete. However, I managed to turn the negotiation into a positive outcome using three main points:

1. The existing relationship, which was built over four years.

2. Emphasising my role as a bicultural person, and therefore the capacity of the company to be able to deliver a successful Australian model but with adaptation to the Chinese culture.

3. Although the Australian company was not able to compete on size, it was able to compete on quality.

The first point was communicated with few spoken words from either party. The second was largely discussed along the lines of communication and past examples of failed Western companies. The chief negotiator on the Chinese side was educated in Australia through Australian secondary and tertiary systems. She confided in me how hard she found communicating with Americans and Australians when I was not there. Because of her exposure to Western tertiary education, she was aware of the concept of cultural differences. She also specifically pointed out the endless examples of unsuccessful Western companies in China. She emphasised why they must have a Chinese model modified from an Australian model. They must not use a pure Australian model.

I use that example to argue that the Glass Wall Effect may lead to the most dangerous of all behaviour because it is not easily recognised and does not become obvious until damaging results appear. When this happens, relationships and trust are damaged, causing difficulties for future cooperation that might lead to permanent separation.

A Foster's general manager with previous experience working in Taiwan was imbued with a false sense of security in managing mainland Chinese staff. Both the management and the executive fell into the trap of the Glass Wall Effect. The executive used his past knowledge from Taiwan in dealing with mainland Chinese, thinking there was just one Chinese culture.

Senior management were even more in the dark because they thought the executive's language skills gained in Taiwan were just enough to manage the mainland Chinese employees. To the contrary, the mainland Chinese did not trust him because of his language skills, and kept information and knowledge away from him. His Taiwanese knowledge was totally out of place in mainland China.

He did not understand that Taiwan and mainland China differ dramatically in many aspects of culture, with the major cause of differences being the Cultural Revolution. The core concept of the Cultural Revolution was to eradicate traditional Chinese culture and to implement the Communist doctrine.

Mainland Chinese under the Communist regime gave up many traditional Chinese values that Taiwan maintained, and Taiwan Chinese have embraced many strong Western cultural, political and business influences through close association with America, in particular, since the Second World War. On the other hand, during the same period mainland China was totally closed to the West until a change in attitude began to emerge slowly about 30 years ago, accelerating in the 1990s.

The existence of the glass wall blinded the general manager who had been in Taiwan from accurately seeing mainland Chinese behaviour and prevented him from addressing issues accordingly. Equally, the company's selection process of appointing personnel who spoke the language and had experience in Taiwan (or other geographically close Asian countries) was a result of the Glass Wall Effect. Of course, that was not the only selection criteria.

Assumptions that previous international experience will lead to success in China pose dangers because such individuals may not be capable of seeing China in a different way. It is natural for people to seek similarities between cultures to protect their comfort zones, but such perceptions and the use of stereotypes almost guarantee a poor result.

Common comments among those who have dealt with people of other cultures include 'People are people', 'People are all the same', 'The Chinese are the same as us in business because they want profit and so do we'. Perhaps these comments appear to be reasonable on the macro level, but at the micro level they do not help. They create a Glass Wall Effect in cross-cultural communication.

Chairman Mao said: 'A blank sheet of paper is better. Pictures can be drawn on it.' People without prior knowledge are less likely to bury their heads in the sand and pretend they cannot see problems when they encounter them, and therefore there is less chance of a Glass Wall Effect occurring. The only way to overcome the problem is to clearly recognise the possible cause of such an effect and face any new culture without predetermined stereotypes.

Interpreters in cross-cultural communication

In communication processes with Chinese, interpreters are always used, but this in itself can be a major cause of misunderstanding. Figure 2.2 illustrates the situation when one interpreter is used for communication between

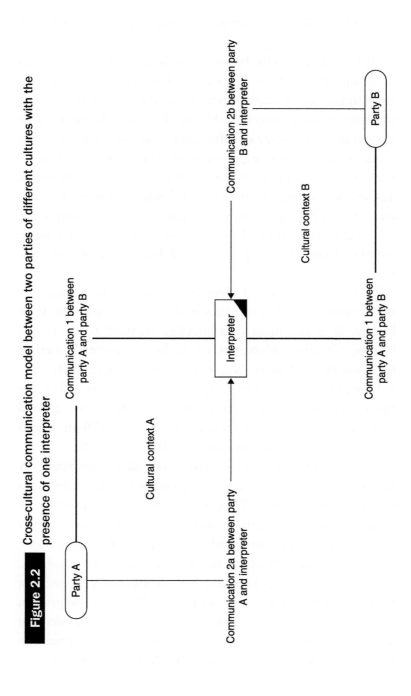

Figure 2.2 Cross-cultural communication model between two parties of different cultures with the presence of one interpreter

party (A) of Western culture (A) and party (B) of Chinese culture (B).

To have to translate between English and Chinese means that one negotiation process is now composed of two communication processes where the interpreter is the core element of both processes. He or she controls the flow of information, accuracy of information and more importantly the accuracy of meanings being sent through each end of the parties. This is no doubt a challenge for any individual. Those with strong cultural understanding of both Western and Chinese business cultures are clearly going to achieve the set target better than those who do not. (This of course, assumes that the interpreter has a high level of language skills in both languages.)

It is common when Westerners arrive in China for negotiations that they are allocated, or locate, an interpreter locally. It is the most cost-effective method to overcome language barriers. However, when the interpreter has no or little understanding of Western culture, it is unlikely they will be able first to understand, and second, to translate the full and correct meaning of all messages. This is often ignored as people tend to use technical knowledge as the scapegoat because it is more obvious and tangible.

In addition, the interpreters are often provided by the Chinese party and most commonly are employees of that organisation. They have good understanding of their organisational culture, and working knowledge of their organisation, colleagues, and products. On the other hand, they know very little about the Western party and products.

A third problem is that Chinese are culturally bound not to tell anyone they do not understand. Therefore even when they encounter issues, phrases and words they do not understand, they will not acknowledge that or seek clarification for fear of losing face. Therefore, for Western negotiators, to engage an interpreter who has the full understanding of Western business culture is far more effective than using who is provided.

Fourth, an effective communication process with interpreters relies on both sets of communicators. People who are not exposed to working in different languages do not have the skills needed to work with interpreters. They often speak a paragraph before stopping to allow the interpreters to interpret. For inexperienced interpreters, or informal situations where interpreters do not, or do not have time to, write notes, translations cannot be complete. Points are often missed or misunderstood by other parties.

However, this will create the situation where two interpreters are used, as illustrated in Figure 2.3 when each party engages their own interpreters. This complicates the intended single communication process of the negotiation and turns it into three communication processes. Ideally, both interpreters have equal expertise of both cultures and language skills. The third process of communication between the two interpreters is where messages and meanings are clearly transferred between Westerners and Chinese. However, that circumstance is rare.

Differences in the expertise of individual interpreters engaged by Westerners and Chinese are unavoidable and therefore an imbalance in the spoken communication processes is likely to occur and miscommunication is equally inevitable. By understanding this, Western companies will also understand the importance of engaging good interpreters who have competent cultural knowledge of both Australia and China, on top of their competent English and Chinese language skills.

The previously mentioned differences in communication styles of high context and low context cultures, between Chinese and Westerners, are posing a barrier for speakers to achieve full awareness of the misunderstandings, which in

Figure 2.3 Cross-cultural communication model between two parties of different cultures with the presence of two interpreters

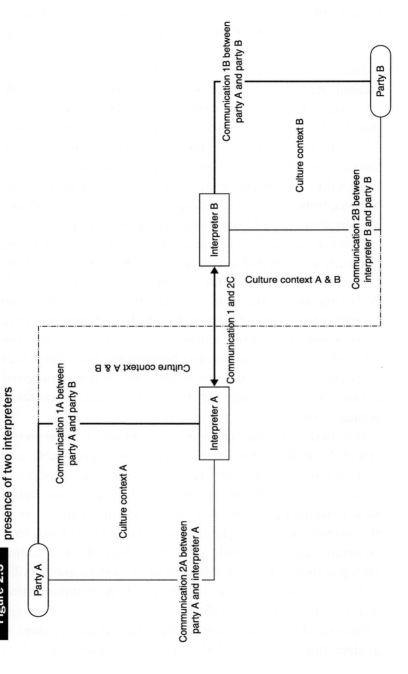

turn leads to their failure to attain the goals of the negotiation (Coupland, Wiemann, and Giles 1991).

The importance of interpreters cannot be emphasised enough, because half-baked cultural knowledge or none at all and incompetent language skills of both English and Chinese, are likely to confuse issues rather than clarify them. Too often we hear 'Chinese all speak English.' Chinese all try to speak English, but very few speak good English with a sound understanding of Western business culture. They cannot understand the nuances and implications; hence they miss the real meaning covered by Western business people. These culturally branded phrases and terms flow with the language, consciously or not when used.

On a recent trip with an Australian delegation to China, one member of the other party had an Australian tertiary degree and citizenship. Theoretically speaking, she should be translating for the Chinese and I should be translating for the Australians. But because the company with which we were negotiating was known to me for many years, this formality was soon abandoned. Negotiations progressed positively, but we still stumbled on several miscommunications simply because the different Australian system could not be understood and there are no similar comparisons in the Chinese system.

When we finally concluded the negotiation positively and signed an agreement, my Chinese counterpart commented how important cross-cultural communication is and how my presence helped. She also commented on previous negotiations with a US firm, which was less successful despite having a Chinese person on its team.

Communication issues are constant in the process of conducting business with Chinese. Even after dealing with Chinese for some time, experienced Westerners will revert to their normal low context communication style at some stage subconsciously. This is inevitable because we are branded by the culture we grow up with. According to the latest neural research, we are hard-wired in the ways we communicate.

One long-term client of mine who has been to China many times with me and left much of the major negotiation to me, periodically expresses his disbelief at the Chinese partner's behaviour: 'I don't understand what he is doing. It doesn't make any sense.' I found myself in the position of using expressions such as, 'This is not what he meant', 'Please understand from his position as Chinese, or Australian' to both sides constantly.

For another client, when the Chinese expressed their conscientiousness in projecting sales figures for the reason of implied responsibility (which is more cautious than Western businesses projection), the Australians interpreted that as 'The Chinese are not willing to do a feasibility study'.

As a consultant, I need to be on high alert for these types of communication hurdles at all times. These situations re-occur sometimes on a daily basis.

References

Adler, R. B., and G. Rodman, 2000, *Understanding Human Communication* (Harcourt College Publishers, USA).

Chaney, L. H., and J. S. Martin, 2004, *Intercultural Business Communication* (Pearson Prentice Hall, Upper Saddle River, New Jersey).

Chung, M., 2008, *Shanghaied: Why Foster's Could Not Survive China* (Heidelberg Press, Melbourne).

Condon, J. C., and F. S. Yousef, 2002, 'Communication perspectives', in S. Little, P. Quintas, and T. Ray (eds), *Managing Knowledge* (Sage Publications, London).

Coupland, N., J. M. Wiemann, and H. Giles, 1991, *Miscommunication and Problematic Talk* (Sage, Newbury Park).

Dwyer, J., 2002, *Communication in Business: Strategies and Skills* (Prentice Hall, Frenchs Forest, NSW).

Hall, E. T., 1976, *Beyond Culture* (Anchor Press/Doubleday & Company Inc., New York).

Hall, E. T., and M. R. Hall, 1990, *Understanding Cultural Differences* (Intercultural Press, Inc., Yarmouth, ME).

Kennedy, J., and A. Everest, 1996, Put diversity in context, *The Secured Lender* 52, 54.

Kim, D., Y. Pan, and H. S. Park, 1998, High- versus low-context culture: a comparison of Chinese, Korean, and American cultures, *Psychology and Marketing* 15, 507–521.

Korac-Kakabadse, N., A. Kouzmin, A. Korac-Kakabadse, and L. Savery, 2001, Low and high context communication patterns: towards mapping cross-cultural encounters, *Cross Cultural Management* 8, 3–24.

Tian, R. G., and C. Emery, 2002, Cross-cultural issues in Internet marketing, *Journal of American Academy of Business, Cambridge* 1, 217–224.

Tse, D. K., K. Lee, L. Vertinsky, and D. A. Wehrung, 1988, Does culture matter? A cross-cultural study of executives choice, decisiveness and risk adjustment in international marketing, *Journal of Marketing* 52, 81–95.

3

The Chung Model: a practical business example

Abstract: This chapter introduces the important theoretical model in cross-cultural communication – The Chung Model.

It goes on to demonstrate how the model may be used in assessing a strategic situation, communication process, negotiation process, a decision making process and how goals may be achieved. This is especially important in a cross-cultural situation. With real case material, this chapter demonstrate how the model may be used by managers and executives.

Key words: the Chung Model, objectives, goals, critical point.

The Chung Model, which I first developed in 2008, aims to provide the understanding, and help the process, of cross-cultural communication. The unique feature of the model is bicultural personnel acting as cross-cultural communicators. The model can be applied to any cross-cultural communication process and explained and demonstrated in a cross-cultural context. It can also be applied to any cross-cultural project to help in decision-making and strategic planning.

Figure 3.1 explains a situation where culture A and culture B are engaged in a communication process. Theoretically speaking, if A and B are to reach their final goal, they may start the process with an objective Critical Point which will eventually be developed into their final goal.

Figure 3.1   The Chung Model

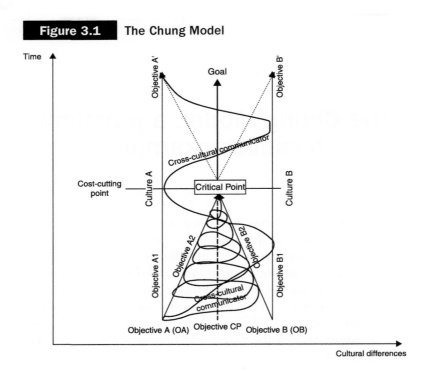

The model acknowledges the cultural differences of A and B, and the initial objectives from A and B can be significantly different. The diagram also illustrates that unless these differences are bridged via a cross-cultural communicator, the gap will remain. Parties may finish with objective A' and B' rather than the goal.

Ideally, objective A1 and B1 will start developing when the cross-cultural communicator attempts to point out the differences between both parties. When the communication process reaches a Critical Point, both parties will consider it as the time of consolidation. This may be the cost-cutting point where, if no possibility of a common objective/goal is likely to be reached, the negotiation/project (seen as a communication process) should be abandoned. This is the situation where objectives A and B are estimated to become objectives A' and B'.

In the case of the Foster's experience in China, objective B1 does not automatically become the new objective, because:

1. The Foster's China operational goal differs from the Foster's goal set by head office. The cultural differences were not recognised at the time of setting the strategy, and the former strategy of entering the market with a consistent, high-quality Australian product rather than one for Chinese consumers, was not suitable for China. The executives who had experience in China understood the country was different to other markets, especially Australia, and therefore new strategies needed to be formulated. Equally, objectives had to be adjusted.

2. The previous goal was to achieve the success of the Foster's brand through joint ventures.

3. It was clear to the organisation that investments in China could not be short term.

4. It was recognised that the focus of the operation should be shifted from production to marketing, but before this objective could be achieved a cross-cultural management structure was needed.

Changing goals

At this stage, communication continues to play an important role in the process. Until 2000, when Shanghai Foster's became fully owned by Foster's Group, OA1 and OB1 existed in parallel with the new goal. Although Foster's Shanghai was a Foster's Group foreign subsidiary in Shanghai by 2006, it could not operate in a vacuum. The hope of Foster's, as well as many other foreign firms, was to run their own business their way.

Despite Shanghai becoming a foreign subsidiary, Chinese Government departments still had an interest in the venture's performance. By now, OA1 (objective of Chinese party) has been modified and so has OB1 (objective of Foster's). Although the Ministry of Light Industry no longer had financial commitments in the operation, staff welfare continued to be of major interest to the Government. In other words, the hope of removing party A to simplify the communication model through a wholly owned subsidiary did not eventuate. Foster's had no choice but to modify its original objective B1.

The operating Chinese environment seriously influenced the new Foster's decision-making process. For instance, cutting staff numbers as part of the new objectives could not have been carried out as planned from the head office in Melbourne. Organisations that enter the Chinese market also enter a 'marriage for life' with the Chinese Government, in one form or another, as long as they remain in China.

An Australian company's Critical Point in Shanghai

Another example of how this model operates is an Australian company based in Victoria, China Corp, which was established as the China arm of Fisher's Group of Companies. This was done to reduce the potential risks of entering the Chinese market. China Corp went to China to look for suppliers of parts.

After two initial trips, both with the assistance of either the local government or the State Government of Victoria, the CEO of China Corp felt it was not moving forward. It found a particular supplier in Shanghai who was happy to supply one line of product. China Corp, however, had a bigger vision as it was looking at the potential of supplying the European market with a number of products sourced in Shanghai that were used in production back in Victoria.

China Corp recognised its major impediment at this point was cross-cultural communication. Its initial approach using casually employed interpreters in Shanghai appeared not to be effective. Other than overcoming the very simple and basic language barriers, the interpreters could do no more. At this point China Corp engaged a China business culture expert as a consultant, acknowledging this was essential if it were to pursue the China path. The consultant specialised in Australia–China cross-cultural business communication.

In addition to having fluency in both English and Chinese, the consultant also had a deep level of understanding of social and business cultures, and how phrases, communication styles and behavioural differences occurred and were practised between Australians and Chinese. The consultant also had broad business experience in both countries in strategy, management and marketing. (It is appropriate to state that the consultant is the author of this book.)

The initial discussions with the Shanghai supplier Honglin were about entering into a more serious collaboration, such as a joint venture. This approach was initiated on the basis that China Corp had no intention of making large capital investments in Shanghai and no plan for a major commitment to set up a large operation there, other than utilising the existing infrastructure of Honglin.

This suited both parties as Honglin was happy to expand without incurring major expense other than in expanding its market base from mainly China to an international market, with Australia and Europe as its primary focus. Honglin had no expertise in international marketing and recognised this shortcoming as a major impediment to its international dream. Honglin also had no capacity financially, nor the vision, to invest heavily in building its capacity, because of its very entrenched culture of an inward-looking and risk-avoiding approach.

Once the communication process started, the consultant acted as the cross-cultural communicator. Very soon the consultant established that the real objective of Honglin (objective A1) was not really a joint venture but simply to obtain more orders through the relationship. China Corp decided this was within its workable range as long as Honglin would enter a joint venture. The rationale of a joint venture at that point was to ensure Honglin made the commitment to a joint working relationship rather than simply trying to obtain extra orders at all costs.

It took Honglin some time to decide whether it really wanted the joint venture. It was going through a stage where the senior manager was retiring and a younger manager was taking over the operation. Eventually the new manager won the argument for the higher risk-taking approach. Through this, Honglin firmed its commitment to collaborating with China Corp.

Honglin and China Corp still had two different objectives but they did agree to work towards one goal, which was to set up a joint venture. The Critical Point in this case was when the younger manager took over from the older manager and committed to go down the path of forming a joint venture. The China Corp experience in relation to market entry strategies is explained further in chapter 5.

The loss implications

For management, identifying the Critical Point by applying the Chung Model and evaluating the cost-cutting point, are essential steps in a successful business operation because they will avoid continuous losses. Many international companies have lost millions, even billions, in China. The question is always asked, 'Why haven't they decided to withdraw earlier?' However, an inaccurate judgement leading to an early withdrawal may result in the loss of a market opportunity.

The brewer Carlsberg, for example, withdrew from China in the late 1990s because it did not want to continue down the path of losses. But the breweries Carlsberg sold were purchased for tens of millions and sold for similar amounts. By 2004 Carlsberg was urged by the international players to re-enter the Chinese market and purchased breweries for hundreds of millions rather than tens of millions. There is a saying that opportunity seldom knocks twice.

Although the unit cost of production is comparatively low in China, this may mislead foreign organisations into underestimating the level of investment funds required. Investments in China are often made on a large scale to try to cover the local market. Cultural differences always extend the time needed to set up projects beyond what might normally be expected elsewhere. These investment factors lead to substantially higher project costs than expected. Therefore, effective communication with shareholders is essential to ensure their continuing strong support.

4

Characteristics of the Chinese in commercial negotiations

Abstract: This chapter provides the theoretical support for negotiation with Chinese. It introduces the topic of face and its importance when negotiating with Chinese. Using case material of Rio and BHP, two large mining companies' negotiation experience, it demonstrates an element which does not always dominate negotiations in the Western business world.

It also introduces the concept of Chinese order of arguments which is very important in understanding the Chinese logic. This is not understood as very few writers make this clear. Without an understanding of this, Western negotiators struggle to understand the Chinese logic and vice versa.

It covers power, gender and approaches to cross-cultural negotiation.

It goes on to introduce the Cultural Capability Theory, a fundamental factor in cross-cultural negotiations. It has the potential of guiding HR firms in their selection process.

Key words: negotiation with Chinese, Rio and BHP's negotiation with Chinese, order of arguments, power, gender in negotiation, cross-cultural negotiation, Cultural Capability Theory, emotional intelligence, bicultural negotiators.

'Negotiation is a common, everyday activity that most people use to influence others and to achieve personal objectives'

(Lewicki et al. 2003). Negotiation is a basic part of our daily life, and human life is a large negotiating table. Negotiation is a common communication process that frequently occurs in business and is defined as a mutual exchange of signals.

Definitions of negotiation

There is no shortage of negotiation definitions. Negotiation is broadly used, from bargaining and haggling to formal negotiating and mediating. It varies from culture to culture (Foster 1992) and in some cultures negotiation can be extended to the establishment of life-long relationships. For the purposes of this book, Fisher et al.'s 1991 definition of negotiation as 'a process of communicating back and forth for the purpose of reaching a joint decision' is adopted.

Negotiation can be a stressful process and most people do not negotiate very well. Investigation of senior-level executives worldwide shows 95 per cent reached sub-optimal outcomes in a realistic business simulation (Thompson 2001). This alarmingly high failure rate should alert us to the need for improvements in negotiation skills among business people, especially when operating in a cross-cultural context.

Negotiation is often ranked as one of the most important skills for global managers to have (Fayweather and Kapoort 1972, 1976). The importance of negotiation has risen dramatically following the increase in business activities worldwide and negotiation processes are becoming more and more involved across cultures. One of the clear effects of globalisation is this greater need for face-to-face negotiations between people of different cultures.

This is more complex than negotiations between people of the same culture (Adair 2003). Negotiators often pay more attention to other factors such as legal systems, political structures, constitutional authorities and other matters to compensate for their inadequacy on cultural-related issues. The cultural factor is sometimes discussed as just one of the elements of these other matters, but is not recognised as a fundamental issue: culture colours and influences everyone's negotiating behaviour.

The increasingly important position of China in world trade raised the topic of negotiating with Chinese to a new level of importance. In recent years, this topic has become increasingly interesting from both sides. Although Chinese universities and publications pay much more attention than Western universities and literatures, the actual business activities suggest that both Chinese and Westerners are equally poor with their negotiation results.

Publications provide an abundant amount of 'tactics and skills'; however they merely provide routines of negotiations and forget that all negotiations are novel (Strauss 1984). Therefore, knowing how negotiations across cultures can be achieved to their utmost effectiveness is the key to success in cross-cultural business.

Bicultural negotiators are the most effective. They are familiar with both cultures in a negotiation (Chung 2008), they are capable of effective communication beyond language skills in both cultures, and can switch between each at ease. This is the key to successful negotiation with the Chinese.

Rio and BHP's long-term win

Cultural differences influence the interpretations of the goals of the negotiating parties, which may differ dramatically from their actual goals. Take, for instance, when Chinese make gestures to Westerners that they cannot agree to certain things because doing so may result in losing face. If Westerners do not understand the significance of this cultural nuance, the negotiation process may be jeopardised or at least encounter difficulties.

As a real example of this situation we can look at the iron ore price negotiations in 2006 between Rio Tinto and BHP Billiton, and Shanghai Bao Steels and other Chinese steel mills. Historically, the international iron and steel market had been self-regulated in that once the leading suppliers and purchasers negotiated and agreed to a price, it flowed on to the rest of the international market.

Japanese and European steel mills had been the largest iron ore purchasers. Then early in 2006, the world's biggest iron ore producer, CVRD of Brazil, negotiated a price increase of 19 per cent with European steel mills for 2006–2007 contracts. This flowed on to contracts signed by both CVRD and Rio Tinto with Japanese steel mills in May 2006.

China was furious when these 19 per cent increases were announced. It had become the world's biggest iron ore user, and the biggest steel producer and consumer. China found itself in the position of losing face politically in that it had failed to perform the role expected of the biggest player by leading any price adjustment. Even worse was that China lost face to the Japanese. China was in a difficult situation. BHP, Rio and CVRD immediately went on to negotiate with other steel mills and locked in 57 per cent of the world market at the 19 per cent price increase, in order to force China into a corner and agree to the new price.

By the end of May, however, China was hinting at possibly opting for the spot market price in order to save face (Wyatt 2006). In the end, China was indeed forced to the negotiating table. But straight after the signing in June, the Chinese media launched a huge campaign denouncing Westerners and Australian companies as 'evil capitalists' taking advantage of China's rapid economic development. This caused major and long-lasting setbacks in relationships between Chinese steel mills and Australian iron ore producers.

An important cultural characteristic of the Chinese is their long-term memory, especially relating to insults and hurt feelings. As this book was being written in early 2009 the world economic crisis was still deteriorating and Australia had reason to be concerned about its iron ore and other mineral exports. China was gearing up for new negotiation of their contracts.

There is a Chinese saying, 'A gentleman's revenge is not late even if he has to wait for 10 years.' The Australian negotiators might have put the negotiations of 2006 behind them. The Chinese will not.

We cannot reverse time nor spin the global dice again as in the movies, but the companies in those 2006 events should have sought advice on the cultural understanding of 'the face issue'. The entire negotiations could have been handled very differently to avoid the negative backlash, and still achieve the desired results.

One Chinese official even said international rules and conventions were violated and commented: 'This will not be helpful in building long-term and stable cooperative relations between suppliers and buyers' (Chen 2006). The China Iron and Steel Association also suggested that 'negotiating rules' were broken during the price discussions and a 'stable long-term cooperative relationship' was clearly not built well enough by the Australian producers (Freed 2006).

What was most humiliating to the Chinese was the loss of face, not the price increase. Australian negotiators are often puzzled by why Chinese negotiators might bargain so hard on the price in a negotiation yet later sign a contract with a different company at a higher price. Price bargaining may sometimes be the smokescreen for the Chinese attempting to tell Westerners of other problems, often simply the issue of losing face (Chung 2008).

Order of arguments in negotiations

Another important impact of cultural differences is how conclusions and supporting evidence are presented. Chinese, being high context culture people, present their supporting evidence first and the conclusion last, to emphasise the importance of the concluding point for which they are arguing. Westerners, being low context culture people, present their conclusion first to be very clear and concise, then the supporting evidence in a logical order starting with the strongest argument.

This distinct difference between low context and high context groups is likely to result in both parties going off on separate tracks without being conscious of this happening. This may cause each party to the negotiation to mistake conclusions for evidence, or vice versa, hence total miscommunication and inability to grasp the main points. This is very significant in the negotiation process, especially when reading between the lines and decoding hidden agendas are also required skills.

Understanding the Chinese

On a micro level, a person's characteristics are determined by their cultural origins. Individual traits also influence the way in which negotiators differ, both across and within cultures. Individuals seek positive social identities in inter-group encounters; therefore they are more conscious of being accepted by others within the same cultural group. At the same time, the same cultural background is usually also the signal of 'you are one of us'; therefore pre-setting of rules can be omitted. With negotiators of a different cultural group, we first have to deal with the 'way in which cultural identities are created and negotiated with others' (Guirdham 1999).

At the beginning of China's open-door policy, negotiating with the Chinese was seen as easy. The lack of language skills (English) and international knowledge was often taken advantage of by Western negotiators. The reality is that negotiating with the Chinese is difficult. Here are some reasons why:

- Coming from different cultures, different rules in negotiations apply. They can catch people by surprise.

- Chinese are generally tough negotiators. Tactics they use may not be identified by Westerners and hence it is only recognised when a firm conclusion is drawn.

- Chinese are new on the international negotiation platform and Westerners often do not recognise them as experienced negotiators; their capacity is often underestimated.

- Chinese are very quick learners and often learn and use the Western style of negotiating to their own benefit.

- China is taking negotiations much more seriously than companies in the West. Negotiation is taught as a subject in most Chinese university business courses. The newer universities are also better equipped, with computer labs for example, to train students.

Problems commonly encountered by Western business people in negotiations are:

- There is no predetermined time for negotiations. They may be long or short, and negotiations that have continued for weeks, months and sometimes years may suddenly be fast-tracked after a banquet with someone who was previously not on the scene. This can be particularly difficult for Western negotiators when they are on a mission and guided by a timeframe.

■ Negotiations with the Chinese are never concluded. When a contract is signed and an agreement is reached, it is not the end of the negotiation. Issues that have been negotiated or not negotiated may surface at any time before or after the signing. Anything is subject to negotiation and renegotiation. Contracts symbolise the beginning of a long-term cooperative relationship rather than steps and details to be followed. When contracts are signed, few details are usually included. This is not a matter of respecting or not respecting a piece of paper; rather, it is recognised that circumstances change constantly and flexibility is essential.

■ Chinese now enforce clauses in contracts only to the benefit of themselves and to put Westerners in a difficult position.

Recognising the difficulties, some people have written books and articles; training courses have been constructed in an attempt to provide a magic wand in negotiations with Chinese. Most of these available tools only address the symptoms, not the cause. Understanding how Chinese operate, and hence formulating tactics to address behavioural differences, will lead to much more effective negotiating.

Such writing on the principles of negotiation styles usually evaluates negotiation techniques in general. However, it is the fundamental argument of this author that in order to formulate strategies for successfully negotiating with Chinese, the first step is to understand the underpinning cultural elements.

Team spirit

The collectivist/individualist paradigm (Hofstede 2001) is another characteristic that may have an impact on how negotiation teams may be formed. The decision-making process is also reflected by this culture. Chinese will often have more people in a negotiation team than their counterparts from Australia.

Chinese culture is a collective one. They do everything in plurals, including doing one job by more than one person. In the Chinese language, there is no plural form of nouns; numbers are added to particular nouns. At times, deliberate vagueness can be tolerated. Chinese teams do not make major decisions on the spot or let decisions be made by individuals. This is seen most obviously when a negotiation team is small, regardless of its members' rank and power.

The value of power

Power is an important element of negotiation and is strongly influenced by culture. Two types of power relationships influence the fundamentals of how people of different cultures negotiate: egalitarian power relationships and hierarchical power relationships.

In egalitarian power relationships, people expect to be treated as equals, and for them the basis of power is their possession of information rather than status. In hierarchical cultures, power distance is closely correlated with position and status (Thompson 2001). This may be extended from a personal level to an institutional level.

Power in a culture can also be measured by power distance (Hofstede 2001). In a high power distance culture such as China – where a degree of inequality between people in society is tolerated, in that a subordinate is perceived as having less power or influence than a superior – it is critical to follow and comply with formality. For instance, many Chinese negotiators with high positions will insist on using an interpreter, even though they speak very good English themselves. Being seen with an interpreter demonstrates their status, rather than simply a practical need.

Gender in negotiations

When forming negotiation teams, it is advisable to carefully study the counterpart's culture beforehand. If they are from a strong masculine culture (Hofstede 2001), in which the dominant gender role pattern is male assertiveness and female nurturance, it would be better not to use female negotiators. If the situation cannot be avoided, female negotiators should carefully perform a more 'feminine' role, even if they are the chief negotiators on the team. They should at least be seen as not so aggressive and tough as males.

This is in no way meant to suggest that females should be submissive members of the team who easily give in. The suggested method is referring to the negotiators' communication styles. In this way the negotiation approach will be perceived as less threatening.

Approaches in cross-cultural negotiations

Win-win is the desirable outcome that all negotiators aim for (Fisher, Ury, and Patton 1991) although Dawson (2003) believes win-win is a myth in negotiation. He says a fundamental aspect of negotiating is that the different parties have completely opposite aims/goals: in international trade, the buyer wants the lowest price possible; the seller wants the highest price.

Chinese books on negotiation present the 'win-win is the best solution' approach as more of a tactic. Still, cases often demonstrate how the Chinese have won negotiations (Jing and Xi 2001). Negotiations of joint ventures, perhaps, are the only possible situations where both parties are interested in one outcome – the establishment of a successful joint venture.

But before that goal is reached, matters of asset values, human resources and control of management are often a major focus of disagreement. It is impossible to complete negotiations of any kind without giving up something in return for getting something. Perhaps beneath this 'myth' of a win-win, mutually satisfactory outcome, contradictory intentions are the cause of failures in joint ventures in China.

The previously mentioned high failure rate in negotiation attracts people to the concept of 'golden keys to negotiation'. Dawson (2003) suggests:

- First, never say yes to the first offer. It raises two negative thoughts in the other team: 'I could have done better' and 'something must be wrong'. Chinese do not say no, nor do they say yes. Either way they feel they are giving away too much, too easily. (See other chapters for more on 'face' and the meaning of yes for the Chinese.)

- Second, flinch. When people make a proposal they are watching for your reaction. Chinese pay more attention to the non-verbals in negotiations.

- Third, avoid confrontation. This is a particular problem for lawyers, whose initial communication is likely to be in the tone of a threat. Get into the habit of agreeing initially and turning it around. Presenting lawyers to Chinese negotiators suggests you do not trust them.

- Fourth, find other ways to make the other party feel they win. Again this is the face factor: don't want to lose face, don't want the other side to lose face.

However, negotiations with Chinese require more than just the ordinary 'golden keys', which are formulated in a Western cultural context. Chinese negotiators are notoriously tough, clever, shrewd, highly skilled, patient, well-trained and professional (Shi and Wright 2001).

Western companies that are part of a transparent, legally structured society may favour legal representatives in their negotiation teams. This is understandable because they would like to avoid unforeseeable legal remedies in the future. However, negotiations with the Chinese may experience the following poor perceptions.

1. A legal approach is still a relatively alien concept. The Chinese legal system has been established gradually, only since 1979. Thus Chinese people may be intimidated by the presence of legal representatives in negotiations, although the new generation of negotiators are rapidly being trained to bring their legal counsel to the table. Even so, most of the time it is doubtful if legal counsel are seen as having more than just decorative value.

2. Lawyers are trained in a one-dimensional 'cause and effect' method of argument. In cross-cultural negotiations, this is a disadvantage because cross-cultural communication is generally multi-dimensional. Furthermore, they are trained to argue that they are right and the other party is wrong.

3. Lawyers are quick at categorising incidents and information. This may create a narrow focus down a

specific path, thus preventing them from seeing the big picture.

4. Lawyers are trained to be critical and so are constantly looking for weak links in an opponent's argument, which prevents them from seeking win-win solutions.

5. Fundamentally, lawyers walk into a negotiation room with a threat. Unless the other party complies, they will demonstrate what the available legal options are. As part of a negotiating team they should enter a room to find out what the other party wants, then compare the bottom-line.

For these reasons, using legal representatives in negotiations is not necessarily wise; and in dealing with the Chinese in particular, great caution should be exercised.

Cultural Capability Theory

A major theory that guides the concept of bicultural negotiators is the Cultural Capability Theory (CCT) (Chung 2008). Cultural capability is defined as an individual's ability to adapt, act, empathise and communicate effectively between different cultures.

In the process of negotiating across cultures, people who are capable of rapidly changing their thought processes and actions when reacting to external stimuli – that is, they can adjust their behaviour in anticipation of subtle changes in cultural context – have a higher level of capability in dealing with cross-cultural situations. Individuals have different levels of capacity when operating in different cultures.

The Cultural Capability Theory contends that a degree of natural talent exists in everyone, for example a talented ballet dancer. Training will improve such natural ability, but because individuals may start from different levels of capacity, the end result of training may vary from person to person. CCT explains such differences in the ability of individuals when dealing in different cultures. Fundamentally, CCT can be supported by personality theories (Blackwell, Miniard, and Engel 2001).

CCT has two dimensions: the horizontal level, an individual's capacity in dealing with multiple cultures; and the vertical level, an individual's capacity for deep understanding in dealing within one particular foreign culture.

There are many specific examples of individuals who had experiences as expatriates. Among the Australian executives of Foster's Brewing (Australia's largest beverage company) who worked in China, some adapted well and began to adjust their behaviour to the cultural environment; others never really adjusted nor liked being there.

One in particular said he had a poor experience in China; that he did not like most things in China, including Chinese food. He was later moved to Vietnam, where he thrived and blossomed. In an interview during this author's research he specifically commented that he even loved Vietnamese food. Another executive who previously worked successfully in Fiji had a poor experience in China, which caused serious management difficulties involving local Chinese staff. His assignment had to be terminated prematurely.

The two dimensions of CCT are often not recognised by organisations. It is often wrongly assumed that if a person is successful in one foreign culture, he or she will be successful in another. An executive of a large Australian corporation had very good relationships with people in a Middle East culture and he was assigned to China. He had no interest in, or adaptability to, the Chinese culture, to the extent that other executives on his team experienced moments of embarrassment while working with him.

A new expatriate may start with a honeymoon period of adapting into a foreign culture, but someone with less capacity to adapt more deeply into that culture will soon struggle as their progress stalls. This is often not recognised by organisations or individuals, because they are inclined to find more obvious or acceptable answers to the problem, such as family difficulties or personal or business conflict with others.

Sternberg's 1986 intelligence theory demonstrates the existence of levels of intelligence (Sternberg et al., 1995). It explains attributes at a biological level of intelligence, which helps to explain how some people can be trained as ballet dancers while others do not progress far even after training. Earley and Ang (2003) suggested that adaptability to new cultures could be defined as cultural intelligence, and they made no apologies for suggesting that individual intellectual differences in adapting to new cultures might be similar to other forms of intelligence such as emotional intelligence, personal intelligence and social intelligence.

Earley and Mosakowski (2004) attempted measurements similar to IQ (intelligence quotient) and EQ (emotional intelligence) to measure CQ (cultural intelligence quotient). Thomas and Inkson (2005) suggested that cultural intelligence is a step beyond emotional intelligence and is the next necessary step in global management practice. They introduced three components of cultural intelligence: knowledge (to understand cross-cultural phenomena); mindfulness (to observe and interpret particular situations); and behaviour (the skill of adapting behaviour to act appropriately and successfully in a range of situations). The components are integrated and build on each other. Interpersonal and communication skills are essential to cultural intelligence.

It is accepted that training will improve an individual's performance but is not a guarantee of top performance.

Some people manage better than others in cross-cultural situations and some training processes may provide the same opportunities, but with different results. Using CCT, we can explain the differences between those who are capable of adapting to new cultures and those who are not. It also allows for the acceptance of individual differences rather than ignoring them.

This raises the question of personnel selection for positions where cross-cultural capabilities are required. Cross-cultural capability needs to be raised to a higher level of strategic human resources management, rather than remaining as just one step of training people with a low level of cross-cultural capability. Globalisation means firms no longer have choices in their dealings with people but have to deal with people of all different cultural backgrounds.

CCT as a theory assists in distinguishing the effect of individual differences when managers are dealing with cultures other than their own. Knowledge of the ability to adapt and handle such culturally different behaviour could be used to guide management practice in successful personnel selection. Concepts of cultural intelligence provide a deeper understanding of human behaviour in cross-cultural settings to further guide management's decision-making processes. Acceptance of CCT places recruitment at a higher level of importance and responsibility in determining the success of a negotiation.

CCT has great potential in guiding policies and processes relating to human resources management. It suggests that individuals with a higher order of capability when dealing in cross-cultural contexts should be given primary consideration for culturally challenging jobs such as negotiation.

An extension of implementing CCT is consideration of the effectiveness of training. The first step is to identify a person whose cultural intelligence is such that they can become a first-class performer. The second is to provide a top trainer with support and resources. The third is a good training program plus effort from the chosen person.

The method of matching key words to a job description is not an efficient way to select personnel with cultural capabilities.

One of the major contributions in this book is the concept of a bicultural person. The solution to bicultural negotiations, that is, negotiations that involve two cultures simultaneously, is to use bicultural negotiators who have the ability to do that. It is an acquired natural skill, which some are capable of, especially with training, but some will always struggle.

The fact that there are so few bicultural negotiators who are capable of simultaneously managing the challenge of integrating cultural dimensions and interpreting different sets of demands and messages, suggests there is obviously a crucial need for appropriate personnel selection in the cross-cultural negotiation process (Benet-Martinez et al. 2002).

Bicultural negotiation experts are fully aware of the particular strategies used by both cultures in negotiations. This has obvious benefits compared with mono-cultural negotiators who are only aware of one side's strategies. For instance, as discussed earlier, Chinese negotiators, being part of a collective culture, are inclined to attend in a collective group of people. Within that team, power level is dependent upon the hierarchical order of its members. At the beginning of a cross-cultural negotiation process, power distance plays an important role in the effectiveness of communication. Parties to the negotiation are likely to establish power levels. Bicultural negotiators are indispensable because they can identify the power structure of the team through experience, knowledge and observation.

Equally, the decision-making process is another difficult challenge for negotiators who are not familiar with the other side's cultural characteristics. Decisions cannot be seen to be made by a specific person because of the collective culture; on the other hand, the person with the highest status or power to make decisions wants such status or power to be confirmed.

This is a difficult equation for Westerners to understand because they want to be clear who makes the decision. The fact that a collective as well as an individual makes the decisions is an oxymoron to them. The highest-level leaders make decisions, but it must be seen as a collective decision-making process. It is impossible to operate within this cultural conundrum unless the negotiator is fully trained and understands precisely how to play the game.

It is important for the Chinese to 'win' at a negotiation or at least be seen as winning. This is because of the need to recognise a higher status winner or 'hero' in their high power distance culture. If the 'hero' is not identified in this culture, the reward system is unable to function. Moreover, when both parties are from a high power distance culture, compromising is likely to be seen as weakness. This explains the scenario when parties are reluctant to compromise in negotiations.

When one party is of a high power distance culture and the other is of a low power distance culture, it is possible for the high power distance team to press for compromise. But when the other party makes a compromise, further compromises are expected to maintain the power distance. The complaint by Australian negotiators that Chinese make fewer compromises is a culturally biased perception caused by a lack of understanding of the Chinese culture and its values.

Making compromises is an essential part of negotiation. In cross-cultural negotiations involving Chinese, the question of compromise is viewed differently. Because of the cultural differences, when one party makes a compromise it is not necessarily appreciated by the other. Often they feel the other party was too pedantic about some minor points but kept avoiding major ones. The low-context cultural nature of Westerners in using fewer and more precise words gives the impression that less negotiation is conducted. Therefore there is less 'haggling' around the issues and less 'negotiation'.

Obviously that would mean less 'compromising'. When compromises are made by the Chinese, with a great deal of effort because of the different culture and values, they may be seen by Westerners as less worthy of the perceptive Chinese value, and vice versa. The role of the bicultural negotiators is to identify these differences and communicate them to each negotiation party (Chung 2008).

Bicultural negotiators are essential in cross-cultural negotiations. They have the capacity to recognise differences caused by culture that otherwise would be missed. Misunderstandings based on this can grow during the course of negotiations, the main danger being the possibility of hurt feelings. As mentioned earlier, Chinese do not forget their hurt feelings quickly or easily.

References

Adair, W. L., 2003, Integrative sequences and negotiation outcome in same and mixed culture negotiations, *The International Journal of Conflict Management* 14, 273–296.

Benet-Martinez, V., J. Leu, F. Lee, and M. W. Morris, 2002, Negotiating biculturalism: Cultural frame-switching in biculturals with oppositional versus compatible cultural identities, *Journal of Cross-Cultural Psychology* 33, 492–516.

Blackwell, R. D., P. W. Miniard, and J. Engel, 2001, *Consumer Behavior* (Harcourt College Publishers, Ft. Worth, Tex.).

Chen, F., 2006, Official urges settlement to iron ore price disputes (Xinhua News Agency).

Chung, M., 2008, *Shanghaied: Why Foster's Could Not Survive China* (Heidelberg Press, Melbourne).

Dawson, R., 2003, 'Secrets of power negotiating', in R. J. Lewicki, D. M. Saunders, J. W. Minton and B. Barry (eds), *Negotiation: Readings, Exercises, and Cases* (McGraw-Hill, New York).

Earley, P. C., and S. Ang, 2003, *Cultural Intelligence* (Stanford Business Books, Stanford, California).

Earley, P. C., and E. Mosakowski, 2004, Cultural intelligence, *Harvard Business Review* 82, 139–146.

Fayweather, J., and A. Kapoort, 1972, Simulated international business negotiations, *Journal of International Business Studies* 3, 19–31.

——, 1976, *Strategy and Negotiation for the International Corporation* (Ballinger, Cambridge, MA).

Fisher, R., W. Ury, and B. Patton, 1991, *Getting to Yes* (Pelican Books, New York).

Foster, D. A., 1992, *Bargaining Across Borders: How to Negotiate Business Successfully Anywhere in the World* (McGraw-Hill, Inc, New York).

Freed, J., 2006, China plays up difference in iron ore shipping costs, *The Sydney Morning Herald*.

Guirdham, M., 1999, *Communicating across Cultures* (Macmillan Business, Hampshire).

Hofstede, G., 2001, *Culture's Consequences* (Sage Publications, Thousand Oaks).

Jing, R., and Y. Xi, 2001, 谈判机理 (*Principles of Negotiation*) (China Machine Press, Beijing).

Lewicki, R. J., D. M. Saunders, J. W. Minton, and B. Barry, 2003, *Negotiation, Readings, Exercises, and Cases* (McGraw-Hill Irwin, New York).

Shi, X., and P. C. Wright, 2001, Developing and validating an international business negotiator's profile: the China context, *Journal of Managerial Psychology* 16, 364–389.

Sternberg, R., and R. Wagner, 1986, *Practical Intelligence: Nature and Origins of Competence in the Everyday World* (Cambridge University Press).

Sternberg, R. J., R. K. Wagner, W. M. Williams, and J. A. Horvath, 1995, Testing common sense, *American Psychologist* 50(1), 912–927.

Strauss, A., 1984, *Negotiations – Varieties, Contexts, Processes and Social Order* (Jossey-Bass Publishers, San Francisco).

Thomas, D. C., and K. Inkson, 2005, Cultural Intelligence – people skills for a global workplace, *Consulting to Management – C2M* 16, 5–9.

Thompson, L., 2001, *The Mind and Heart of the Negotiator* (Prentice Hall, Upper Saddle River, New Jersey).

Wyatt, S., 2006, *Iron Ore Settlement – Comment* (Macquarie Research, Shanghai).

5

A culturally sound entry strategy brings success

Abstract: This chapter discusses the market entry modes of Foreign Direct Investments (FDI), in specific FDI into China. It argues for a culturally suited strategy for the unique market. Joint venture (JV) is suggested over the other methods for China despite the fact it is harder to manage. This is argued based on the necessity of the local Chinese knowledge. With case material of Foster's market entry strategy, this chapter demonstrates suitability of a particular strategy and more importantly necessity of local knowledge when reaching such important decisions. It further emphases the important role of a bicultural personnel.

Key words: investments in China, FDI, joint ventures in China, modes of entry, wholly owned foreign subsidiaries, Foster's market entry strategy to China, bicultural personnel.

Foreign direct investment by organisations is not new, but it has received prominent focus in recent years due to the large flow of funds into developing countries, especially China and India. Research shows the success rate for business investing overseas is often much lower than investing domestically. However, the returns and market expansion are usually the main attractions for multinational corporations to take the path of foreign direct investment.

A much more complex option

Investing in a foreign country is much more complex than investing domestically. Nearly every area of operation and practice will be different in a foreign environment, fundamentally because of the differences between cultures. Culture shapes the behaviour of human beings, hence their decision-making processes, operational patterns, problem-solving, thinking process and so on. Therefore, investments into culturally different environments become highly dependent on the local situation for their success or failure.

China has the largest cultural gap between it and any country among Western nations. Investing in China is often a highly controversial set of contradictions. On one hand, China is very attractive with its 1.3 billion (official) population. On the other, most Western companies know very little about these 1.3 billion consumers. At the same time, the evidence of low prices of goods and labour misleads organisations into thinking that investments can be made at low monetary cost. However, they do not know that investments are often required on a large scale; and the timeframe for any returns is often much longer because of a lack of local market knowledge.

Examples in this chapter will demonstrate this and also what difference it makes when bicultural personnel are used.

Historical overview of foreign direct investment

Organisations pursue foreign direct investment (FDI) generally to seek growth and expansion, when their domestic or nearby markets are small, saturated, crowded and/or limited. Specific foreign markets have the potential to produce a higher rate of return, in the short or long term. For Australia in particular, with its entire market size of about 21 million consumers, pursuing international markets is obviously attractive.

The history of FDI goes back much further than recent years and commercial globalisation. The initial British involvement in continental Europe began as early as 1029–1087 with holdings in France, and by 1860 Britain was the world's largest trading nation. The Dutch had established the Dutch East Indies Company in 1602 in Indonesia to pursue trade and become a dominant European power, while the Portuguese had established a share of world trade and business from as early as 1500 in Brazil.

Investments have been in many different forms, direct and indirect, jointly and separately. But investing in an environment of foreign culture has never been an easy task. Historically, nations have sometimes refused trade initiatives mostly for reasons of protecting national interests. Americans in 1837 and 1846 tried to trade with Japan but were unsuccessful and a British and Chinese trade dispute led to the Opium War in 1839.

The modern challenge of China

Being a huge market of rapidly growing prosperity, China is attractive to multinational corporations around the world. In 2006 it was the second-largest recipient of FDI in the world, according to CIA statistics. For Australia, according to the Department of Foreign Affairs and Trade, China is now its largest partner in two-way trade.

The economic importance of China to the world, including Australia, is clearly shown by rapidly increasing trade figures. China has been Australia's largest trading partner since 2007, according to the Australian Bureau of Statistics. Total trade that year grew 15 per cent to $58 billion. Australia's exports of goods to China rose 17 per cent to $23.8 billion.

Companies from around the world have been pursuing the Chinese market in a more focused manner since the economic reforms of 1978. Inward investment in China in 2005 and 2006 was around $70 billion a year (Davies 2007). However, only a very small number of firms are meeting profitability projections and many others have made large capital write-downs. Most US and European multinational corporations have never made a profit in China, according to Haley and Haley (2006).

The first business challenge for foreign businesses in China is to examine the investment strategies. Why are companies interested in investing overseas, especially when the cultural differences are so difficult to overcome? Apart from the cultural hurdles, there are general issues such as availability and cost of land and raw material; the cost and quality of labour; capital; efficiency of production; access to supporting industries and technology; closeness to existing and potential markets; and the possibility of tax incentives and/or other local benefits. Arbitrage between these factors is a major motivation for organisations to pursue larger profit margins.

These factors can be grouped to determine the homogeneity of countries where investments are made in order to assist the decision-making process (Zhang 2000; Zhang and Zhang 2001). The grouping exercise is one way of helping to improve the chances of success, because similarities usually mean a higher success rate. This assumption generally works better when market similarity exists and the gap in differences is small. For a market like China, this general rule does not work because market differences are mainly determined by cultural differences.

Three waves of investment

Foreign investments into China came in three major waves. The first investment fever occurred in the late 1980s. After the 1978 open-door policy, only the curious and brave companies went to China. I recall translating the joint venture law for a young Canadian entrepreneur who was anticipating selling his motorbike to enable him to invest in China.

'The Law of the People's Republic of China on Chinese-Foreign Joint Ventures' was adopted by the Second Session of the Fifth National People's Congress on July 1, 1979 and was promulgated and became effective on July 8. Although the Chinese Government did allow wholly foreign-owned enterprises under this legislation, it actively promoted the concept of joint ventures, which was reflected in the title of the legislation (Chu 1986). Foreign companies were often under the impression that only joint ventures were permissible for foreign direct investment. Foster's, the world's largest beverage company, was a case in point when it invested in China in the early 1990s.

Between 1979 and 1986, there were 7978 enterprises established using foreign investments. Of those, 7798 were joint ventures and only 180 were wholly owned foreign enterprises (Chu 1986). Through joint ventures, China hoped to not only obtain capital investment but also gain access to Western management skills (which was seen by the Government, and still is today, as of major importance) and new technologies.

In joint ventures it was typical for Chinese firms, especially the rundown ones, to provide the land, existing equipment (often out of date) and employees as part of the deal. Foreign investors typically brought in investment capital, new technology and equipment, and Western management systems and philosophy. Through this process, many outdated state enterprises were upgraded and their efficiency dramatically increased, bringing them much closer to international standards.

The brewing industry was a typical example. In the early 1990s China had 850 breweries (Major 2001), a large number of them unsustainable, and by 2004–2005 only around 250 had survived.

By 2008, the benefit of China's approach could be seen. It now has the world's largest foreign currency reserves and no longer requires huge amounts of foreign direct investment. In 2006, major changes were made to the original 1979 law governing Chinese–foreign joint ventures. The previous tax-free incentive of three years for joint ventures no longer exists. The so-called 'two into one' tax system, which is a straightforward 25 per cent tax, applies to all organisations. This change means more uncertainty for foreign investors, but reflects the current attitude of the Government towards foreign direct investment.

In 2010, the Chinese Government was using the same approach to establish a hitherto non-existent age-care industry. China's population has an increasing percentage of aged people. The Government tells developers, local and foreign, that it does not have the capital funds needed but is happy to support the establishment of a healthcare industry by providing very cheap land. Depending on the specific local government, incentives include tax breaks, reduction of land prices and even free land. In Beijing the facilities are subsidised on the basis of per resident.

Companies have been searching for the correct form of foreign direct investment, mainly because the success rate in general of these investments has not been high (Breth and White 2002; Bruton and Ahlstrom 2003). Foreign direct investment is gaining in popularity, especially on the back of the third Chinese investment wave, which is one of the largest, and so far appears to be producing better results than the first two.

Assessing methods of entry

Books on international business theory always suggest methods of entry should follow a sequence in all foreign investment activities. The sequence involves exporting, international licensing, international franchising, specialised models, and foreign direct investment. Graduate and executive training programs are inclined to include exercises that follow these sequences. However, in practice, other elements such as the companies' financial backing, type of industries, existing business activities, and/or competitors, should also be considered. This is similar to the grouping exercise that allows more certainty. For executives, this is a more tangible way of planning and assessing markets before entry.

More importantly, in this book, the Chinese market is regarded as the number one priority. Rather than considering these options as a sequence of steps, the most important element for China is its cultural difference. Strategies without the input of cultural differences are doomed to fail. The following three major factors (Breth and White 2002) are specifically related to decision-making criteria when entering the Chinese market, based on cultural differences compared to the Australian market:

1. The amount of capital a company is prepared to commit to the Chinese market.

2. The degree of control a company wants to have over its Chinese operations.

3. The company's attitude towards risk-taking and its assessment of the risk in China.

Because of the cheap labour, and sometimes raw material as well, companies form the perception that investing in the Chinese market is low cost. This often leads to insufficient capital, which causes projects to be discontinued or additional budgets having to be sourced. The false impression is caused by an imbalance of income and price distribution. Although the earnings of a waitress can be 20 per cent less than in Australia, a cup of coffee may cost two or three times more.

The truth is, on two levels, China can be a costly place for investments: the length of time it takes to do business with Chinese and the scale of investment required.

Because Chinese do business on the basis of relationships and trust, it takes some time to build a workable relationship. Generally a minimum of 18 months to two years is required for people starting on their own. A bicultural consultant who speaks the language and understands the culture can greatly reduce the time to six to nine months, allowing for trips back and forth to visit people in China.

As a bicultural consultant myself, I have worked with clients for whom I was able to secure contracts on the first trip but that type of success is usually based on an existing personal relationship before an important visit. Generally, when I work with clients on overseas visits to China, I improve the efficiency by between 200 and 300 per cent.

The scale of operations in China often surprises Westerners, especially Australians coming from a country of 22 million people. It can take some time to get used to dealing with the zeros relating to numbers, such as those for employees, products, orders, etc. The Chinese numbering system does not translate easily with the English system, as in thousand, ten thousand, one hundred thousand. Chinese has a separate character for its first four digits (up to 10,000), then starts counting by ten thousand, one hundred ten thousand, a thousand hundred ten thousand, and so on. When the number reaches ten million a new and totally different character is introduced. It is easy in a translation to lose or add a zero by mistake.

The degree of control

The degree of control is an important consideration when companies decide on the form of market entry into China. A fully owned subsidiary means companies have more say in final decision-making, whereas a joint venture can cause difficulties in the managing process. But the real issues are how the corporate structure affects operations and whether companies can manage in China on their own.

The attitude of a company towards foreign investment can also affect their investment policies. For example, in the first wave of China investment fever, funding in millions of dollars was common. In the second wave, when investments involved tens of millions, companies such as Foster's felt the pressure to follow suit and rush in, fearing being left behind.

The urge for speed was understandable for two reasons but was also a double-edged sword: other international competitors were getting into the market and grabbing the spotlight; and those not there, such as Foster's, were losing investment opportunities rapidly because their competitors were buying up breweries and the required capital was increasing rapidly. On the other hand, the rush and pressure caused long-term problems flowing from not being well prepared before entering the market.

In the third wave, investments are required in the hundreds of millions. Carlsberg is a good example. It entered the market roughly at the same time as most other major international brewers in the early 1990s, purchasing Chinese breweries for between $10 million and $20 million each. By 2003, its major purchases of Chinese breweries were in hundreds of millions. For companies the size of Foster's and Carlsberg, several million dollars only represent a very small percentage of their total investment portfolio.

For them and many international companies, China in the 1980s and 1990s was simply an unknown quantity and a mystery, and the feeling was that investments counted in the millions represented very small risk. The total of $250 million that Foster's officially wrote down over several years represents less than 1 per cent of its total foreign investment portfolio. Foster's finally left China in 2006 after 13 years. Perhaps this small percentage was one reason the company paid insufficient attention to its investment and operational strategies in China right from the start of planning its entry.

How joint ventures lessen the risk

The reason a joint venture is such a popular form of entry for international companies is that it can reduce the level of risk – financial, political and cultural. A joint venture reflects an unwillingness to commit the huge amounts of capital required by a wholly owned foreign enterprise and also, in the Chinese market particularly, recognition of a lack of knowledge and cultural awareness that only a local partner can provide.

The essential ingredient for a successful joint venture is the ability of each partner to provide what the other cannot. By pooling their resources, skills and experience, the partners are able to create a more successful business operation than if each were to operate independently.

Companies use joint ventures as a market entry strategy to optimise their overall approach to international expansion (Beamish and Karavis 1999; Lin and Germain 2000; Guillen 2003). In reality, there is no consistent proof of the success of joint ventures despite their popularity. One of the costs associated with setting them up is the search for an appropriate local partner and integrating the pooled assets of the partners (Madhok 1997). In China this is especially critical because the majority of foreign companies have had trouble working with their partners because of cultural differences.

For example, what really surprised Foster's was that China's breweries were mostly owned by the Ministry of Light Industry, which formed joint ventures between individual local breweries and various international breweries. This meant the same joint venture partner was forming different joint ventures with its own competitors. Foster's found its trade secrets were being passed on to its competitors via the Ministry link. This was difficult for managers to deal with and they had no experience or training in managing in these circumstances. Simply, they were out of their depth in trying to find strategies to combat the situation.

Joint ventures can be an attractive form of market entry in China for several reasons:

- They require a smaller capital commitment than a wholly owned foreign enterprise.
- The Chinese Government offers attractive tax concessions.
- There is less political risk because joint ventures are not wholly foreign owned.
- The Chinese partner can deal directly with Government organisations that may seek to restrict or interfere with the operation (in many cases, these organisations are the joint venture partners).

- Joint ventures can be a cultural bridge between the foreign company and the Chinese market, thereby facilitating the development of products that meet specific local needs.

However, the 2006 changes to the law on Chinese–foreign joint ventures may change the thinking of some organisations. The main difficulty for foreign investors is the different interpretations of investment policies by different local governments. For example, a new joint venture foreign university received incentives in the higher education industrial park in Suzhou, in the form of buildings and staff to service them. When the university grows, it simply asks the local government for more buildings.

It is difficult for a Westerner to understand that these incentives are not written down, in a contract or any other way. The university can give no clear indication how long the buildings will be available to the foreign company.

But it does understand that the industrial park is built to accommodate universities, and being the first foreign university with a Chinese partner, the company is confident it will not be asked to leave in a couple of years. This is a hard concept for a Western mind, and especially a legal practitioner, to understand. The foreign university in question appointed a Chinese academic with mainland background to head its campus. He has successfully persuaded his senior executives in the foreign country to allow him to operate under the local government regimen.

The drawbacks of joint ventures in China include:

- Limited control over the joint venture in the market.
- The resources supplied by the Chinese partner, such as the workforce, factory or raw materials, may not be of desirable quality.
- Standards may not be acceptable.

- Disputes may arise over such issues as whether the end product is to be sold locally or exported.

- Whether profits can be repatriated or whether they must be ploughed back into the venture.

- The likelihood of being forced to use the Chinese partner's inefficient distribution channels.

- The foreign company realising, after having signed the joint venture contract, that it has chosen the wrong partner. There are many Chinese organisations looking to enter joint ventures with foreign companies because they can offer capital and technology, and management and marketing skills. Great care must be taken when screening and evaluating prospective partners.

Wholly owned foreign enterprises, on the other hand, enable companies to retain complete responsibility and control over all aspects of the business (Davidson and McFetridge 1984). Such enterprises avoid the conflicts in interests and objectives with local partners that often characterise joint ventures, enabling the foreign company to pursue its own goals free from internal interference (Tse and Pan 1997). This form of entry has been gaining popularity in the third investment wave.

Foreign companies in China are gaining more experience, which they believe reduces their need for a local partner to smooth the way when increasing resources and financial commitments to local operations, and in gradually increasing their proactive role and risk-taking in the market. Companies that choose this strategy may have had some years of poor experience in managing joint ventures in China.

Foster's is a perfect example of this. In 1997, the Australian-based brewer reviewed its investments in China and decided to sell the Guangdong and Tianjin joint venture breweries and keep the one in Shanghai. In Shanghai, Foster's was gradually buying back the 40 per cent shareholding of the Chinese partner. By the end of 2001, Shanghai Foster's was a fully owned foreign subsidiary. But the fact it never reached the profitability break-even point was evidence that this form of investment holding is not the key and only factor to success.

The blame game hides the truth

I argue, controversially perhaps, for the opposite. My experience and research suggest that failures have been mainly because of the deficiencies of Western companies in managing organisations in China, whether involved in a wholly owned foreign subsidiary or a joint venture. I rarely hear self-analysis of how and why the joint venture management was not successful. Instead, the finger is always pointed at the joint venture partners. The most common remark is 'the Chinese partner interfered with management and operation'. To my knowledge, no Western organisation has ever said, 'we had no idea how to manage in China'.

The real truth behind failure in managing organisations – be they joint ventures or wholly owned – is the lack of capacity to understand the differences between cultures and not having successful strategies to manage these differences. This can only be achieved by bicultural personnel who have the understanding of both sides of the cultural divide. Without this, the differences cannot even be identified, let alone rectified.

Another reason for the argument in favour of joint ventures in China, regardless of the format, is that no organisation can escape controls of one form or another. Under the Chinese system of government it is better to have a partner who understands that system well and will collaborate and assist.

Wholly owned foreign enterprises are also said to be the preferable option because of the greater possibility of profit increases as a result of efficiency associated with management autonomy (Woodcock, Beamish, and Makino 1998). However, they are only likely to be more profitable if substantial knowledge of the local market is not required (Vanhonacker 1997). Therefore this is almost near impossible for foreign enterprises in China unless they have the support of a bicultural management team.

In China, because of the very high level of cultural differences, many multinationals have found that local market knowledge cannot be obtained without the participation of local partners. Foster's was certainly fully aware of this and the joint ventures approach was seen as a necessity in its initial entry decision.

The argument of interference also seems to miss the fundamental point that a company operating in China cannot avoid constant dealings with Chinese organisations, especially Government at multiple levels. Joint ventures with an equal amount of equity and a sharing of management control tend to have a higher rate of success; performance tends to suffer when the foreign partner exercises dominant control (Avruch 1991).

Foster's certainly tried to dominate the control of all its joint ventures, something its Chinese partners did not appear to object to in most cases. This dominating pattern in management, operations and marketing was not recognised by Foster's as a contributing factor to failure. And it continuously pursued further control. The real tragedy of Foster's was that it never reflected on finding out what was going wrong. Even during the research period for this book, I observed the same mistakes being repeated.

The Foster's entry and growth strategy

The Foster's entry strategy for China was aimed at seeking growth and expansion at an international level. As a part of this international strategy, Foster's ventured into the Middle Eastern market in the 1980s on a small scale. Although some would question this move, at least it provided Foster's with much-needed international market experience. Senior executives then investigated some Asian countries, including Indonesia, Malaysia and Singapore as well as China. On a social-cultural basis, China was a favourite and its potential for 1.3 billion customers was extremely attractive.

In the late 1980s and early 1990s, China's per capita beer consumption was expected to grow quickly and match the 3 per cent growth rates of other Asian countries. The size of the beer market in China was predicted to overtake the United States by 2002 and become even larger than Germany's, according to the feasibility study by Foster's. This has proved to be correct. The Chinese beer industry became, and still is, the fastest growing in the world and overtook the US in 2003 to become the world's largest beer market.

The decision to establish joint ventures in Shanghai, Guangdong and Tianjin strategically positioned Foster's to cover the entire country. The market for Foster's Shanghai covered the heavily populated and relatively affluent Yangtze delta region (which includes the city of Shanghai). The Guangdong joint venture was established to exploit China's fastest-growing province as well as to serve Hainan Province, Hong Kong and Macau. The Hainan market came with the Princess Brewery, Foster's Guangdong partner. Foster's Tianjin joint venture was located in one of China's largest cities, one of the three direct-municipal cities at the time.

(Direct-municipal cities are under direct guidance of the State Council and have the same status as provinces.) A major objective was to use this as a base to penetrate the lucrative Beijing market, about 100 kilometres away. The initial attempt to purchase a brewery in Beijing had failed.

To keep capital commitment to a minimum, all three joint ventures were to rely on existing regional breweries, which Foster's believed could be transformed into efficient operations. Foster's also wanted to use existing breweries so as not to delay its market entry into China and give its foreign competitors a head start. Foster's purchased additional land with each of these breweries, to provide scope for future expansion and protection against inevitable escalation in land prices.

Importance of local knowledge

Foster's recognised that entering the Chinese market would be a learning exercise and that success could best be achieved initially through smaller operations. Furthermore, by establishing joint ventures, it would benefit significantly from the Chinese partner's knowledge of the domestic market, which Foster's could never hope to match. In particular, Foster's could take advantage of its partners' knowledge of existing distribution channels, their ability to source skilled labour and raw materials, and their expertise in dealing with the various levels of the government bureaucracy. This proved to be largely the case.

All products from the joint ventures were to be sold within the Chinese market and none exported until after 2002. At management level, mistakes were made in areas such as sacking joint venture partners' existing sales staff in the hope of achieving distribution the Foster's way.

The goals of Chinese and venture partners are often diametrically opposed (Png 1992). The foreign partner sees China as the world's largest potential market and a cheap source of labour and raw materials. The Chinese partner seeks to raise the level of managerial skills and technology with a view to increasing exports and earning foreign exchange.

In 2009, Chinese organisations were mostly seeking access to foreign markets, knowledge and experience, rather than technology as in the 1980s and the 1990s. Chinese are quick learners, and are not frightened to learn from anyone and any culture. This fast learning curve in all sectors has no doubt contributed to China's rapid economic development, achieving in 30 years what the West managed to do in 100 to 150 years.

The Chinese partners in the Foster's joint ventures were expecting new machinery, Western management techniques and quick profits. Apart from the Western management techniques, which were not well accepted by the Chinese staff anyway, the Chinese partners were disappointed. Tianjin Foster's Brewery Limited was a joint venture with Wheelock, a Hong Kong investment firm, and Tianjin Brewery. Wheelock's contribution to the joint venture was capital investment. Foster's also hoped for the possibility of future marketing development. But Wheelock lacked knowledge of the beer industry, especially in China, although its initial selection as a partner was based on the perception that Hong Kong companies have a good knowledge of the Chinese market.

Foster's found out the hard way that this is not necessarily so. Chinese culture in China is unique to itself. There is no generic 'Chinese culture'. This is another example of the necessity of bicultural personnel. It is not just a simple matter of being 'Chinese' and speaking the language, and certainly overseas Chinese are not qualified automatically because of that. This is covered further in other chapters.

Success of a joint venture is also based on a large number of business factors (Luo 1995), such as product quality, pricing, sales force marketing and flexible terms of payment. Industry structure, partner selection and timing of market entry are significant moderators affecting the relationship between business strategy and joint venture performance.

The industry structure in China was specifically commented on by many executives at Foster's, with it being described as a 'low level' industry operated by people from a less-educated background. This is because the level of government funding for light industries, which include breweries, is of less importance than for heavy industry such as iron and steel. Credits were poorly managed by wholesalers and industry manufacturers. It was also noted that change management and time were required to adjust the industry for the better.

Nevertheless, full credit must go to the industry's effort, largely because of the contribution by foreign breweries, for current results: the Chinese beer industry has gradually moved up to operate at world standards. Those brewers who do not make the effort to survive are forced to close down. Today, all those that survive can produce world quality products. Larger groups such as Qingdao and Yanjing are not only competing in international markets with its products but also in the stockmarket.

Chinese role is omnipresent

As stated previously, no organisation should hope to escape the important role played by Chinese Government organisations, both as active participants and influencers of performance in joint ventures (Osland and Cavusgil 1996). Many executives at Foster's noted this important role while others expressed a lack of understanding of their own roles as well as those of the Chinese.

When Australian managers discovered their Chinese partner was also the partner of a competitor, it was often a big shock. To the Chinese, this was very normal, because a Ministry can form as many joint ventures with as many foreign investors as it sees fit. An even bigger shock to Foster's managers was when Chinese staff moved from one joint venture to another.

At Shanghai Foster's Brewing Ltd, a Chinese manager disappeared one day. He had been moved to another joint venture, also owned by the Ministry. The Australian management was not told why, or where he was moved to. The Ministry's view was that it could choose to move staff to where they were most needed. Staff were not only moved from one joint venture brewery to another, but also from one industry to another, because each Ministry administers several industries.

In the Western business environment, information about a specific company is regarded as trade secrets and should be kept within the organisation. Giving information to competitors is unethical. But in China there are no secrets and it has to be assumed that everyone knows everyone and everything in the industry. Talking about industry-related information with people within the industry is seen as building relationships and networks. After all, usually one Ministry owns all the competitors; the Ministry of Light Industry owns 850 breweries.

Information exchange is not unethical because the breweries are not really competitors to each other. In fact, they help each other at times such as lending their labels to each other when necessary. These fundamental differences in business practice highlight how Western and Chinese business people differ. What Westerners see as unethical, Chinese see as normal business practice and therefore there is nothing to worry about.

The Foster's review of its investment position in 1997 was clearly related to the fact that the 'China' venture was not profitable after four years. The fact that the then CEO had little idea how the China market worked was directly related to this decision. He was reported to have told the first general manager in Shanghai to 'just make a profit', which would show he had little idea how long that would take in China.

Foster's was unable to sustain consistent heavy losses (according to one executive's notes, as high as $42 million in one year). The review by the board in 1997 resulted in a decision to sell the Guangdong and Tianjin breweries and to buy out the Chinese partner in the Shanghai brewery. In the meantime, the international strategy continued to be developed and soon Foster's ventured into Vietnam and India. Today, Foster's no longer owns any breweries in Asia. It owns a brewery in Fiji, which has long been a training ground for brewers.

That a large part of the China decision was because the Chinese partner was unable to sustain its financial contributions, is understandable under the circumstances. The partner, the Ministry of Light Industry, only invested in the joint venture by contributing the brewery and the workforce that went with it. The Ministry had no expectation of contributing capital at a later stage. This would only be understood by bicultural personnel.

Other major factors in the decision were based on management operations. At Foster's head office it was recognised that a fully owned subsidiary would operate more efficiently and effectively. Foster's pursued a gradual increase in its shareholding to increase its level of control. It is not difficult to comprehend that investment decisions are not a single-factor process. They are complex, involving accurate information and decision-making (Daft 2001). For China, it is even more complex because of cultural differences.

By the late 1980s the downturn of beer consumption in the Australian and British markets had forced Foster's to seek growth opportunities elsewhere in the world. As mentioned previously, the Middle East and Asia were investigated. The Middle Eastern market was not pursued because of its Muslim culture. Although Foster's was exporting a small amount to India, the discouraging foreign direct investment policy of the Indian Government gave little reason to pursue that market.

A preliminary investigation of the Chinese market began in late 1991 and entry followed in 1993. At that time, Asia was considered by the then Foster's CEO, Ted Kunkel, as 'one of the last remaining blue-sky options for brewers'. China represented an integral part of the Foster's Asia strategy as it sought to build a global brand image (Breth and White 2002).

The opportunity began when officials of the Ministry of Light Industry (owner of 850 breweries at the time), were on a state visit to Australia. It is an example highlighting the culture of Chinese business and how much it depends on relationships rather than text-book investment strategies. Foster's was asked by the Prime Minister's Office to host the Chinese Minister. Consequently, he invited Foster's to visit China.

In late 1992, Foster's Brewing Group set up a taskforce at board level to oversee its strategy for entering the Chinese market and Foster's China was established. It marked the beginning of a business adventure in China that lasted about 13 years.

References

Avruch, K., 1991, 'Culture and conflict resolution', in K. Avruch, P. W. Black and J. A. Scimecca, eds, *Conflict Resolution: Cross-Cultural Perspectives* (Greenwood Press, New York).

Beamish, P. W., and L. Karavis, 1999, The relationship between organizational structure and export performance, *Management International Review* 39, 37.

Breth, R., and M. White, 2002, An examination of the joint venture market entry option in China: A case study of an Australian company's international marketing operations in China, *Journal of International Marketing and Exporting* 7, 114–130.

Bruton, G. D., and D. Ahlstrom, 2003, An institutional view of China's venture capital industry explaining the differences between China and the West, *Journal of Business Venturing* 18, 233–259.

Chu, B., 1986, *Foreign Investment in China – Questions and Answers* (Foreign Languages Press, Beijing).

Daft, R. L., 2001, *Organisation Theory and Design* (South-Western College Publishing, USA).

Davidson, W. H., and D. G. McFetridge, 1984, International technology transactions and the theory of the firm, *Journal of Industrial Economics* 32, 253–264.

Davies, K., 2007, China's investment watch, *Organisation for Economic Cooperation and Development. The OECD Observer* 260, 19.

Guillen, M. F., 2003, Experience, imitation, and the sequence of foreign entry: Wholly owned and joint-venture manufacturing by South Korean firms and business groups in China, 1987–1995, *Journal of International Business Studies* 34, 185–199.

Haley, U., and G. Haley, 2006, The logic of Chinese business strategy: East versus West: Part 1, *Journal of Business Strategy* 27, 35–42.

Lin, X., and R. Germain, 2000, Predicting international joint venture interaction frequency in U.S.–Chinese ventures, *Journal of International Marketing* 7(2), 5–23.

Luo, Y., 1995, Business strategy, market structure and performance of international joint ventures: The case of joint ventures in China, *Management International Review* 35, 241–264.

Madhok, A., 1997, Cost, value and foreign market entry mode: The transition and the firm, *Strategic Management Journal* 18, 39–61.

Major, B., 2001, Factors affecting malt and barley selection in the Chinese beer market, *10th Australian Barley Technical Symposium.*

Osland, G., and S. Cavusgil, 1996, Performance issues in US–China joint ventures, *California Management Review* 38, 106–130.

Png, M. L. H., 1992, Equity joint ventures in the People's Republic of China: Problems that continue after more than a decade under the Open Door policy, *Case Western Reserve Journal of International Law* 24, 589–630.

Tse, D., and Y. Pan, 1997, How MNCs choose entry modes and form alliances: The China experience, *Journal of International Business Studies* 28, 779–805.

Vanhonacker, W., 1997, Entering China: an unconventional approach, *Harvard Business Review* 75, 130–136.

Woodcock, C. P., P. W. Beamish, and S. Makino, 1998, Ownership-based entry mode strategies and international performance, *Journal of International Business Studies*, 2nd Quarter, 25(2), 253–273.

Zhang, C., and M. Zhang, 2001, Public administration and administrative reform in China for the 21st century, *ASPA on-line Virtual Conference*, Panel #44 of ASPA 62nd Annual Conference, Newark, New Jersey, 27.

Zhang, X., 2000, Motivations, objective, locations and partner selections of foreign invested enterprises in China, *Journal of the Asia Pacific Economy 5*, 190–203.

The mindset of culture and its impact

Abstract: This chapter discusses the market entry point of the Chinese market. A very important part of understanding the Chinese market is to understand its unique structure – a socialist centrally planned economy with open market characteristics. Therefore the entry strategy must be culturally suited for this unique market. It discusses the necessity of market research. However unless the method is culturally suited, it would not be effective. With real current case material this chapter demonstrates the importance of a bicultural consultant and argues it is the only way that organisations may overcome the cultural barrier effective.

Key words: financial loss, cultural difference, market research, FDI, socialist centrally planned economy, potential market size, labour costs, large scale of capital investment, culturally suited strategies.

We meet people of different cultures who react and behave in a culturally specific manner. Because culture programs our minds, it is the core and the cause of why people do not understand each other. So many Australians over the years have said to me, 'I just don't understand what the Chinese are on about.' So many of my fellow Chinese say, 'These foreigners don't think the same way as we do. They don't understand us.'

Most failures experienced by cross-national organisations are caused by the neglect of cultural differences, according to research (Pan, Vanhonacker, and Pitts 1995). High levels of failure have been observed in many studies, especially on joint ventures, throughout the 1980s and 1990s (Beamish 1999; Li and Tsui 1999).

Financial loss focuses the mind

The financial loss associated with full or partial failure is considerable. It is estimated that between 37 and 70 per cent of international joint ventures are not successful (Pothukuchi et al. 2002; Haskins and International 1989). A survey by the international consultancy AT Kearney showed that more than two-thirds of companies surveyed were unprofitable (Ellingsen 1999).

Culture has only become important in international companies since it was recognised as a cost to business. Culture is important, as Pape (1999) points out. The trend may not be towards a common global business culture but towards business tribes each sharing an individual culture. This is probably due in part to the difficulty in defining, measuring and quantifying cultural costs. There have been many attempts to put cultural differences into a framework of this nature.

It has been argued that where the host country is a high context culture (Hall 1990) and has a less-structured legal system, investing organisations, particularly if large and inflexible, should try not to pursue non-equity-based modes of entry (Brouthers 2002). To date, approaches measuring cultural differences have not been totally satisfactory (Lu 2002). Therefore, the concept of adding cultural differences to potential costs has been a challenge because of the difficulty in producing uniform systems of variables for accurate measurement to determine the exact cost.

The proliferation of cross-cultural businesses in China has attracted the attention of many companies with aspirations for growth. The problem for small-market industrial nations with small local companies (that is, small by international standards), that seek growth in China's comparatively vast market, is that losses can be crippling to their domestic operations. Investment failures are usually attributed to factors such as poor entry strategies, a lack of resources and inadequate demand for the product or service. But these are surface-level symptoms rather than the real causes of failure.

What can be argued is that if cultural differences had been taken into consideration at the strategic level, these symptoms may not have surfaced. For example, if the cultural differences between the home and host countries' consumer behaviour are identified and measurement of procedures put in place, failures can be prevented. Costs can be saved from more efficient and effective communication and actions. Mistakes can be avoided. Projections can be closer to reality if cultural differences are identified, and therefore strategies can be set in place for the actual level of consumer demands. This avoids the costly shock of realising the poor correlation between predictions and actual figures. Further, companies often fail to take opportunity costs into consideration.

Market research must be best possible

In the case of Foster's, strategies sketched out at its Melbourne head office did not reflect the reality of the Chinese market. Research was carried out by large consulting firms who sold reports with endorsed brand names. No one really questioned how the research was done and how data was collected. In the 21st century, the availability of data in China has improved dramatically from the 1980s and the 1990s. Even so, secondary data only has reference value.

In the early 1990s when Foster's purchased an expensive research report from a Hong Kong firm, not only the data and the quality of its real value was questionable, but even worse, part or all of it was the same report sold to other international breweries. International competitors competed in the same city, Shanghai for example, with very similar strategies based on the same report. It is a very good lesson as to why companies should compile reports by engaging their own consultants rather than buying reports from large firms, especially those with big brand names.

China has a distinctly different economic structure to the majority of destination countries for foreign direct investment (Zhu and Dowling 1994) and it is part of its very different business culture. This structure is more complex than the general understanding of China as a centrally planned economy. It has a unique structure involving a hierarchical order of enterprises, the result of the centrally planned economy, based on its five-year plan which resulted in certain industries being listed as more important than others for each five-year plan. The first and the second five-year plans had focused on heavy industry and so did the fourth five-year plan, which caused serious imbalance (Ma 1990). The measure of value used in China is based on the gross industrial output, which forms the base of its planned economy.

The use of this measure has been necessary because of the size and scale of Chinese enterprises as well as the planned economy (Wong 1987). These are the major characteristics of a socialist planned economy in which the means of production is publicly owned (Ma 1990). Enterprises are state owned and funded by the state from budgets based on a five-year plan. These plans ensure and promote the development of the national economy, raising the standard of the people's material well-being as a whole. It is important for foreign investors to understand this and to consider the effect on the structure of the distribution system. This system was established on the basis of a centrally planned economy.

A major part of any investment relies on the supporting system. The above two areas (the centrally planned economy and government allocated financial resources) of distinct differences in China are specifically related to its contemporary socialism culture which was based on traditional Chinese culture, Soviet socialism culture and socialism ideology. Not understanding this background will result in strategies that cannot be effectively implemented. In 2010, although many aspects of the Chinese market have changed, its centrally planned economic structure is still in place. For each five-year plan, there is usually a different focus on an area of development.

Corporations must give the awareness of cultural differences a high priority at the strategic level. Where differences are considered after an entry strategy has been decided, adjustments are necessary during the process of implementation. This means existing strategies are often ineffective. But had cultural differences been considered early at strategic level, their influence would have had an impact on investment decisions.

Among many companies that have not performed ideally in China, the decision to enter the market was often based heavily on potential market size and labour costs. In reality, the pervasive cultural differences mean the Chinese market structure is often very foreign to multinational companies. Consumers are very different in their tastes and buying habits. For instance, in China they purchase small quantities of goods more frequently, rather than large quantities at longer intervals. As well as eating different food to Western consumers, Chinese prefer beer with a less hopsy taste, which is why most international breweries in China today sell mainly light beers.

Preparation is a long-term process

The investment process is likely to be long term. The size of the market requires large investments and this reality often catches organisations off-guard in terms of capital requirements. Generally, preparation to penetrate the Chinese market takes an average of two years. This is mainly because of a relationship-based business structure in which Western companies are required to 'get to know' their Chinese friends first before doing business together. This involves back-and-forth trips to China, usually four times a year. Often Western business people, who do not see a tangible result, consider travelling as a waste of resources.

Small companies, particularly from Australia, that cannot make the capital commitment to these preliminaries, often are forced to abandon projects. At other times, projects are rushed into to save costs and therefore preparation is poor and plans are not well thought out, which impinges on future projects. It could be argued that Foster's selling the joint ventures in Guangdong and Tianjin fell into this category.

By adding consideration of cultural differences at the investment strategy level, decisions will need to be made differently. If the issue is a lack of capital commitment, the entry strategy may be abandoned entirely to avoid financial losses. It is advisable that human resources policies generally reflect the culture-focused strategy so consistency is provided to operations in order to achieve targets (Chan 2003).

It is common for companies to rush into China (Pan, Vanhonacker, and Pitts 1995) without thorough planning so as not to miss opportunities. But correct and accurate information collection (Ehrman and Hamburg 1986) plays an essential role in planning processes. In China, because of its many cultural differences, there is a danger that incorrect information is collected, and the planning process generally takes longer than in countries where cultural differences are fewer.

Not only is China much more complex than other markets, it is also very different. This makes it even more essential that companies do their homework. They must engage in active research themselves by using their own employees or engaging their own consultants. Purchasing reports from external brand-name consultants can be perceived as being more reliable and valuable; easier to obtain and less work than the company doing the homework itself; and if things go wrong (common in the case of China) no one internally has to take the responsibility. In reality, this is seldom true.

The truth is, reports endorsed with a brand name are often disappointing, have no real content, only rely on secondary data, are written by consultants who have no knowledge or experience of the Chinese market, and the interpretation of data is often incorrect and therefore the conclusion is not usable.

Companies, especially large ones, usually have the financial capacity to pay for top-rate research. But with China, a top brand-name report does not guarantee top-rate research. In the early days of economic reform, secondary data was rarely available. Official Government data was mainly for propaganda purposes and had very little real economic value. Secondary data has only become available in recent years. It is more reliable, because of the method of collection, source and coverage, but it should only be considered for its reference value. This is especially the case when data is only mined via the Internet. It is often collected by people with little or no knowledge of China or Chinese businesses.

It is difficult to acknowledge that the initial planning by Foster's was thorough. The board's decision on entry was made in late 1992 and acted on in 1993. Market research was often carried out by either Austrade (the government agency that assists Australian exporters) or casual student researchers. Furthermore, without research infrastructure, it was difficult to determine the quality of any research done. It is reasonable to conclude that the very limited research achieved should not have been used for major decisions without confirmation of the results. It is also fair to say the entry decision was rushed and therefore difficult to execute properly, which probably led to major operational difficulties at a later stage.

Culturally suited strategy a winner for Australian company

China Corp is a small Australian firm that wanted to pursue the Chinese market. This ambition was only pursued when the company decided to engage a bicultural consultant, a decision made after the managing director had made two trips to China without the support of a consultant.

His first trip was with the City of Latrobe in Victoria, Australia, when councillors arranged to visit its sister city, Taizhou, as an annual friendship activity. His original comment on this trip was a 'waste of ratepayers' money'. As a result, he went again by himself initially to source a supply of parts for his home production in Victoria. On the second trip he engaged an interpreter on a casual base, which he found extremely limiting.

After the second trip he decided not to bother with China until he engaged the consultant (the author of this book). His decision was based on the analysis that effective communication without the assistant of a capable person was not possible. The consultant took some time to learn the real needs of the company and understand the business and its industry. This was recognised as important by the director.

In the following year, China Corp proceeded to expand its business in China by establishing a joint venture with an existing supplier. China Corp identified a niche market in the nail-production market – EPAL (European Pallets Association) a not-for-profit industry body governing European pallets. They are a special size certified by the association for quality assurance purpose. EPAL nails are also certified for pallet production.

The process of obtaining certificates is lengthy and costly. The quality requirements are high and the testing procedure is strict. The pallets are repairable and recyclable. There is an open system of a pool of pallets that allows manufacturers, freight forwarders and other users to purchase their own pallets and exchange them in the process of transferring goods. The current pool has about 350 million pallets and, on average, anything between 60 and 80 million pallets are produced every year. The EPAL nail market is estimated to be worth $2 billion.

Based on this information, China Corp prepared to enter a joint venture with a nail supplier to obtain the EPAL licence. China Corp could bring its contacts in Europe, the potential of obtaining European customers, its knowledge and know-how in obtaining the licence. The Chinese partner could bring the joint venture knowledge, skills and experience in nail manufacturing.

The consultant carried out all the primary negotiation between the director in Australia and parties in China, mostly on the phone and Internet. The process started in early 2008 and soon the consultant discovered many complications on the Chinese partner's side. The joint venture could not proceed because the partner did not have proper land and building certificates. In short, the factory the partner built was illegal. The proposed joint venture concept could not proceed.

China Corp decided to set up a wholly owned foreign subsidiary, still collaborating with the Chinese partner. A new factory was required, which was found in a neighbouring city in the outer suburbs of Shanghai. All paperwork was contracted out to a local Chinese consulting firm because it specialised in this type of service and was located in the same city. The firm knew the local government officials on a personal level, which proved to be effective. Being in the same city, the firm was able to transport documents promptly.

By mid-2008, China Corp's director and the consultant went to Shanghai to proceed with setting up the factory. According to Chinese law, the legal identity must be present for many of the procedures, such as opening bank accounts. On that trip the director got the feeling that the local government did not consider the investment was very important because of the amount of money involved, although the government officials he met were all very polite and helpful.

Fast-tracked at the local level

Doing business in China can be full of surprises, especially at the local level. Returning to Melbourne, the consultant continued communicating with the Shanghai partners and other business went on as usual. By early 2009, the global economic crisis hit the world economy. China, a manufacturing powerhouse of the world, immediately felt the pinch. When the Australian director and the consultant returned to Shanghai and visited the office of the local government officials, the officials said all foreign investments would be fast-tracked because of the slowdown of inward investment.

The deal was effected there and then. An official rang another department to establish whether all required documents were in place. Finding one particular document was missing, the director rang the office in Australia. The time difference meant the document could not be faxed immediately. But the director promised the following day. The official rang the chief of the other department and suggested the business licence should be issued to China Corp.

The official said he would visit the department personally and suggested the director and the consultant should also go. They all set off in separate cars, by separate routes. By the time the director and the consultant arrived, the government official was already there. The business operation certificate was issued the following week.

The time taken to establish this project was extraordinarily short. On average, to build a relationship with a Chinese organisation and then to establish a joint venture usually takes a minimum of two or three years. For China Corp, the foreign subsidiary was established just over a year after the first trip the director and consultant made to China.

This chapter has shown how a company's strategy must be suitable for the culture of the Chinese market, and how the assistance of a bicultural consultant is crucial and effective. The company saved about two-thirds of the time generally taken by organisations to get established, and saved probably $80,000. It also saved the opportunity costs, which are often overlooked. For an organisation to wait three years for a project to come to fruition may result in losing the opportunity to competitors. These costs may amount to hundreds of millions of dollars. As mentioned in another chapter, Carlsberg entered the Chinese brewing market in the late 1980s and early 1990s with investments of tens of millions dollars. Having no success, the brewery withdrew. By the late 1990s, it realised the importance of China and it re-entered with investments in the hundreds of millions dollars. The opportunity had passed to competitors. Yet often lost opportunities are not recognised and therefore not measurable by a tangible amount.

References

Beamish, P. W., 1999, Establishing a successful joint venture: Moore Business forms in Japan, in P. W. Beamish, and A. E. Safarian, *North American Firms in East Asia*, (University of Toronto Press, Toronto, ON, pp. 49–71).

Brouthers, K. D., 2002, Institutional, cultural and transaction cost influences on entry mode choice and performance, *Journal of International Business Studies* 33, 209–228.

Chan, J. L., 2003, *China Streetsmart* (Pearson Prentice Hall, Singapore).

Ehrman, C. M., and M. Hamburg, 1986, Information search for foreign direct investment using two-stage country selection procedures: A new procedure, *Journal of International Business Studies* 17, 93–116.

Ellingsen, P., 1999, Dreams fade to red in the Middle Kingdom, *The Age* Melbourne).

Hall, E. T., 1990, *The Silent Language* (Anchor Press/Doubleday & Company Inc., New York).

Haskins, D., and S. International, 1989, *Teaming up for the Nineties – Can you Survive Without a Partner?* (Deloitte, Haskins and Sells, New York).

Li, J., and A. Tsui, 1999, Building effective international joint venture leadership teams in China, *Journal of World Business* 34, 52.

Lu, J. W., 2002, Intra- and inter-organisational imitative behaviour: Institutional influences on Japanese firms' entry mode choice, *Journal of International Business Studies* 33, 19–38.

Ma, H., 1990, *Modern China's Economy and Management* (Foreign Languages Press, Beijing).

Pan, Y., W. R. Vanhonacker, and R. E. Pitts, 1995, International equity joint ventures in China: Operations and potential close-down, *Journal of Global Marketing*, 8, 125–149.

Pape, W., 1999, Socio-cultural differences and international competition law, *European Law Journal* 5, 438–461.

Pothukuchi, V., F. Damanpour, J. Choi, C. C. Chen, and S. H. Park, 2002, National and organisational culture differences and international joint venture performance, *Journal of International Business Studies* 33, 243–266.

Wong, C. P. W., 1987, 'Between plan and market: The role of the local sector in post-Mao China,' in B. L. Reynolds, ed, *Chinese Economic Reform – How Far, How Fast?* (Academic Press, San Diego, CA).

Zhu, C. J., and P. J. Dowling, 1994, The impact of the economic system upon human resource management practices in China, *Human Resource Planning* 17, 1–22.

7

Mistakes to avoid in managing multicultural teams

Abstract: This chapter discusses cross-cultural management and human resources management issues when operating a business in China.

This chapter makes a major theoretical contribution to the cross-culture management and human resources management. It highlights mistakes made using case material from Foster's.

It makes the distinction between the mainland Chinese and overseas Chinese. This is important especially in doing business with mainland China. Business activities today have a strong focus on mainland China. Failing to distinguish between mainland Chinese and overseas Chinese may cause management and other mistakes which can be vital for businesses.

It also discusses the possible issues with expatriates which includes: stability, consistency in management policies and managing Chinese with the understanding of Chinese culture, hence use the Chinese style (but suitable for JVs). Further it is crucial to understand the uniqueness of expatriates' positions and realising the difficulty of overcoming psychological barriers in the process.

Key words: managing cross-cultural teams, mainland Chinese, overseas Chinese, stability of management team, training, cross-cultural management, consistency, Chinese systems, Chinese styles, expatriates, managing Chinese teams, joint venture.

Cross-cultural management in China is crucial to success. Companies often struggle to manage divisions, sections and subsidiaries because of the important role cultural differences play when workplace teams involve Australians, Chinese and people from other countries. Many organisations believe that wholly owned foreign subsidiaries can avoid the issue of managing Chinese in China, but they overlook the reality that operating in China means cross-cultural management issues will arise regardless of the ownership structure of the organisation.

The important distinction between Chinese

This chapter looks at the management of a multicultural global team and managing Chinese in China. Problems can occur regardless of whether companies employ Australian expatriates, or local or overseas Chinese. The distinction between mainland Chinese and overseas Chinese is very important in the effective management of organisations in China. No previous study has clarified the importance of this distinction.

The common mistake of relying on overseas Chinese as the bicultural personnel means their inadequate cross-cultural capacity can lead to missed market opportunities. Businesses need to recruit truly bicultural personnel and properly manage multicultural teams as soon as they establish operations in China. Failure to do so is a common cause of failure in cross-cultural management.

Increasingly, multinationals recognise the importance of cultural difference when it comes to managing organisations in different locations. Lawson (2002) suggested that by not recognising this, the efforts of Australian managers wanting to work with Asians has not achieved as many success stories as there might have been. Indeed, comic situations have occurred when cultural differences have not been observed.

The effect on performance

The challenge for Australian managers, as for other nationalities, is to understand the culture and use this as a basis for conducting business and managing Chinese staff in China. This cross-cultural competency directly affects the performance of many multinationals. Professor Andre Laurent, of INSEAD, Paris, observed: 'Managers who readily accept that the cuisine, the literature, the music and the art of other countries run parallel to one another, must also learn to accept that the art of management differs in other countries.'

The first challenge for Australian expat managers is to realise there are, indeed, strong cultural differences between Australia and China, and they are reflected in the behaviour of employees. Regardless of ownership of an organisation, there will always be Chinese employees working in a subsidiary or branch in China. Therefore, learning how to manage Chinese staff is an essential part of holding a management position in China.

We can use the Foster's China experience to demonstrate how important it is for Australian managers to first understand the differences between the cultures, then to be able to manage across cultures. To understand certain Foster's management activities, it is necessary to first understand the company's strategies. Foster's China was heavily focused on production, clearly demonstrated in the structures of its three joint ventures.

This was strategically planned by head office in Melbourne, based on the belief that China was backward in technologies. This is understandable because Foster's Group originated mainly from Foster's Brewing, which was developed from several brewing companies but primarily consisted of Carlton & United Breweries staff. In short, the largest profit-making source for Foster's was making beer; hence its culture of brewing production dominated operational strategy.

Top-level management had a strong technical focus and there was constant heavy financial investment in infrastructure and upgrading plant and machinery. In China this was also seen as necessary because the Shanghai plant was relatively out of date. Equally, it was felt necessary to get the Quandong and Tianjin plants up to the same level to achieve consistent products.

On a day-to-day management level, there was much more frequent communication between China and the technical section at head office. This indicated a very close involvement of Melbourne operational people in China activities. The principle behind this was to ensure beer produced in China was of an international standard of consistency of quality – Foster's standards. It was under such strategic guidelines that Foster's China management evolved.

Stability of management personnel

China, however, is a totally different market to the rest of the world's markets. Managers assigned to positions in China had no Chinese experience. They had to start learning the basics of culture and then business culture, as well as the day-to-day running of the business. For expatriate managers, settling into a foreign country and managing a business is a challenge in itself, without the added difficulty of dealing with an 'alien' culture when they had little or no past experience to draw on.

At Foster's China operations, managers were generally given three-year contracts, not nearly long enough for them to learn the culture, settle in and then perform. In contrast, Japanese companies are noted for giving contracts for four or five years and do not expect full performance until the third year (Copeland 1987). Some companies even allow expat managers two years to learn their positions and familiarise themselves with the cultures of the host country.

Given that anything from nine months to two years has been suggested, an average of 18 months would be reasonable. Therefore, a reasonable time before Foster's China managers might be expected to perform strongly would be three to three and a half years at the earliest (18 months to adjust plus two years to produce results).

It is reasonable to suggest that managers who held their positions for three years (and not all achieved that) were on the verge of their best performance. If sufficient time were allowed, expatriate managers should be expected to start producing results at three and a half years or at the end of a four-year term.

Training before being sent on assignment tends to reduce the time needed to adapt. Copeland (1987) suggested that Japanese who received training took only a few months to adjust. Blackman (1995) noted that a small number of very large multinationals have trained their staff for three to six months in preparation for China. This training was specifically aimed at reducing the time needed to adapt and therefore reach a high performance level sooner.

As for assisting expatriate managers to adjust to a cross-cultural management environment, research has shown a powerful correlation between inter-cultural sensitivity and training, regardless of whether the training was pre-departure or upon arrival in China (Kaye and Taylor 1997).

Foster's managers did not receive sufficient training to enable them to reduce their adjustment time significantly. The courses that were provided were mainly for language and a few people received tuition in culture. Expats were busy with their work, getting ready to leave for China, and sorting out personal and family issues, so many of them did not even attend all the classes.

The general manager at the Shanghai joint venture in 2005 had a previous four-year appointment with Foster's in Guangdong in the early 1990s. When interviewed during research for this book he had been in his position for 18 months and was confident in his ability to manage the brewery. The brewery had already shown significant signs of improvement and production was returning to a historical high.

These observations make it reasonable to suggest that expatriate positions should be for a minimum of six years, which was, indeed, suggested by several former executives at Foster's during research. The frequent rotation of managers simply created a series of repeating events where trial and error ruled.

The local employees' cultural interpretation of this short-tenure approach was that Foster's was showing instability and insincerity about its intentions in China, leading to concerns about job security and low staff morale. The speedy sale of the Guangdong and Tianjin plants confirmed local employees' concerns and when Shanghai Foster's was fully converted to a 100 per cent subsidiary, some staff protested against the decision in the hope of being taken back by the Chinese party to the original joint venture. A Chinese manager recalled:

For about a month, staff protested. It started as soon as we announced the change of shareholding and continued to the very end. They protested strongly. Many nights they continued until one o'clock in the morning. The reason was because it was a joint venture before there was the Chinese party and Foster's (sic). Once it became wholly owned, the Chinese party was out. All management issues were dealt with by Foster's only. If the wholly owned entity decides to sell, they would pay all their staff out. Local staff needed ongoing jobs. Even the Shanghai government would intervene. Organisations must maintain a balance.

The locals also felt that a three-year posting was not long enough for an outsider to learn and understand how to manage the breweries in a Chinese context. They were aware that learning a new culture and how to live and work within it was a relatively long process, and that each individual had a different management style, which took time for staff to understand and adapt to.

It also took a long time for expatriate managers to learn how to manage local Chinese employees. When staff went on strike in Shanghai, production stopped for two weeks. The Chinese human resources manager dealt with the situation using a Chinese approach. A local manager commented: 'Australians did not know how to deal with labour movements. They could only offer more pay, but did not understand that money was not the only motivation. We did it differently. We did home visits instead of purely offering money.'

This culturally different approach is identified by McDonald (2004), and can only be applied if management has the knowledge to manage local staff. Other studies highlight specifically that for Chinese staff, building relationships is very important for successful managing across cultures.

Consistency important in cross-cultural management

Tianjin was the only joint venture to have only one general manager under Foster's between 1995 and 1999 (from start-up to sale). Shanghai by 2005 had its sixth general manager in 11 years. Guangdong had four general managers between 1993 and 1999. Such senior management change inevitably brought instability. A new general manager meant new systems and new management styles. Not only did a general manager need time to adjust to his new position, but staff also had to adjust to new systems and styles. Instability was heightened by senior management changes also resulting in other personnel movements, including sales and marketing people and interpreters.

For the Chinese staff, stability was extremely important: 508 (the official number) who went with the Shanghai party to the joint venture were accustomed to the state 'iron rice bowl' guaranteed employment system and many did not wish to join the joint venture for fear of losing this stability. Staff were given the choice by the Ministry of Light Industry of remaining in the joint venture or leaving. All who stayed made the choice in expectation of a better future. One typical Shanghai comment in an interview was:

> The employees who decided to stay with the joint venture had a great deal of confidence in it. General managers were changed frequently, but there was a kind of united feeling between all the staff. The employees said they were in it together. We were united,

could not break up. Even after Sebastian came, he made some changes (but) was still OK.

Other international companies have done things differently in China, which has generally been appreciated by the staff involved. KSB, a German joint venture, had a general manager who got on well with the Chinese. When he was due to leave after three years, Chinese staff petitioned head office for him to stay, and he did, for another six years. He eventually left KSB and set up his own consulting firm in China.

Chinese systems, Chinese styles

As mentioned, one of the major objectives of attracting foreign direct investment to the beer industry was to introduce modern Western management systems. This concept was being widely accepted and practised in the early 1990s (Purves 1991).

The acceptance of the Australian management systems being introduced was clearly acknowledged by the Chinese during research for this book. 'The Australians have brought very good management systems and good training to the Chinese,' one Shanghai manager commented. What is questioned here is the appropriateness of the actual process and the effectiveness of a non-adjusted management system.

Foster's tried to select managers from different cultural backgrounds. Three main groups were employed to manage the joint ventures: overseas Chinese with good language skills and limited cross-cultural skills; Australian expatriates with a background of working in Asia/China as well as having language skills; and expatriates of Anglo-Australian backgrounds with no language or cross-cultural skills.

In comparing these groups, the research found different styles among managers in all three. One general manager, Stewart Luk, had a Singaporean Chinese background and held a European qualification, an MBA from INSEAD. His practical experience was largely in Singapore, although he worked for Heineken in Asia.

Luk said he learnt most of his management skills from his father, who had a depth of experience in small private enterprise. 'My management styles are very open. I let people come into my room and talk to me; very strict but open.' However, this was not the view of his Chinese staff members. He was labelled 'a tyrant' by one of them.

He was primarily responsible for Tianjin, which was recognised as a successful operation by many management staff. Luk's open style of management appeared to be very hierarchical and structured, which was not always appreciated by Chinese staff, although the high power distance culture supports the hierarchical culture. However, the collective and harmonious nature of the culture does not support individual differences. Chinese staff simply stayed away, blocking the chance of communication about any disapproved behaviour. It does appear, however, that his management style was adjusted according to the people he was managing. An Australian commented:

> In Tianjin it was a guessing point because Stewart Luk was very much a sales and marketing type and I was the technical guy. In terms of position . . . he was more than happy to leave all running of the brewery operations to me and he would not interfere at all, not much, he never got away with it (and) he would look after the sales and marketing and it worked fine, because there was no conflict of interest.

In Shanghai, Luk's style of management was also accepted by expatriates. In his case it could be acknowledged as being an effective style. Luk put it this way:

> You need to be very experienced in China; if you are not, you are seen as very different. You must be able to understand the culture . . . what culture you must be able to communicate. As a general manager you need to communicate with a lot of people below you.

Head office understood that this leadership style was appropriate at times; for example, Luk worked extremely well with his deputy general manager, who was a local Chinese, as a team in Tianjin. He was moved to Shanghai for a different primary purpose: to put discipline and a framework in place. A Foster's executive commented:

> We took Stewart Luk out of our Tianjin brewery and brought him to Shanghai for lots of reasons. We believed strongly in a localisation policy. We reduced about 17 or 18 expats across three breweries down to two or three. We also wanted someone with a strong administrative history and background in the role rather than an operational person, such as a brewer or marketing person. We wanted someone who was sort of a seasoned old warthog and who was not going to get pushed around by the Shanghai mafia in our business.

Contrary to this, the Anglo-Australian managers with no language skills and little training in cross-cultural skills appear to have enjoyed the most successful period of management. They managed to form more comfortable mutual relationships with local employees. Their management styles were accepted as different, as being Australian and not Chinese, but as long as they made attempts at cultural links, they were accepted.

The effort of learning Chinese and the culture was much appreciated by the local Chinese. Many concessions were made to improve cultural understanding; it was the level of effort that was appreciated. Perhaps that was because the cultural gap was so large that locals had not expected Australians to make any real inroads. However, the level of acceptance for Anglo-Australian managers and overseas Chinese managers was different. The Australians' small efforts were appreciated but overseas Chinese were expected to fully understand and behave in the local Chinese manner.

Other leadership style pointers among individuals were that some maintained a more superficial relationship in the belief that different operational systems were easier to introduce; others believed that having closer relationships with the local Chinese would enable the joint venture to run more smoothly. An expatriate who worked in China in the early days commented:

> I managed my team differently from how Michael had done. He chose to get quite close to them personally. He was trying to start up the venture, start up the brewery, and he had a different task to mine. I saw it as my job to teach them how to manage. I didn't adopt any particular style to do it differently for individuals, but I was fairly open with them in terms of my own personality and what my expectations were of them. I'd tell them, if they did things wrong I'd tell them (and also) if they did things right, and had put some systems in that were probably new to them.

There was virtually no expression of resistance to management changes from any management personnel, although there were differences in the speed of accepting and taking up the changes. A totally different view was expressed by local employees, who certainly had resisted the changes.

It is worth noting the cause and effect of different leadership styles and how the process of management was affected. As mentioned, the leadership styles of expatriates with no language skills were all accepted without obvious contradictions; the leadership styles of expatriates with language skills and cultural skills were questioned at times; and certain overseas Chinese leadership styles were not appreciated.

It can be concluded that a more democratic style of leadership was more acceptable to the local Chinese than an authoritarian style. Littrell (2002) argued that the Chinese are more accepting of an authoritarian style of leadership, and this is supported by Hofstede's high power distance theory. Yet the research for this book found the contrary, that local Chinese clearly prefer a more democratic style.

This has been confirmed over and over again with many other companies as well.

Expatriates' psychological barriers

Expatriate managers often find adjusting to Chinese culture a challenge, because they have to deal with a very different way of life and perform in an unfamiliar work context (Selmer 2000). In this process of adjustment, psychological limitations in the ability or willingness to understand, accept or adopt the norms of a foreign culture can be the major barrier for expatriate managers working and living in China, according to Selmer (2000). The cause of this psychological barrier may sometimes revolve around basic human needs.

Maslow's hierarchy of needs (Davidson and Griffin 2003) suggests that for all people, certain basic needs must be satisfied first. Behaviour differs among cultures, but the requirement for food, for example, is the one basic need of everyone. In the early days of the joint venture in Shanghai, many notes were recorded discussing the need for improvements in canteen facilities and in the quality of the food. It is common in Chinese organisations to have a subsidised canteen that provides food for all staff members. The quality is an important motivator.

Food was equally important for the Chinese and expatriate staff. Not having familiar Western food for long periods drove people to desperation from time to time. An expatriate in Shanghai recalled:

> For the foreigners it was out in the middle of nowhere; absolutely nothing Western there at all. A hard place to work, no TV. Every weekend we used to go to Macau just to eat. Just after I moved into that house by myself back in the early days, I was going home one night in a taxi and I went past this place that sort of looked a bit like a Western supermarket. I thought, wow, so I got home and jumped on my bike and rode back. It had the big light boards out the front and sort of looked like a mini 7-Eleven. It was just full of crap, nothing in there that was interesting at all, so depressing.

What was often not understood was the degree of psychological problems caused by what appeared to be relatively minor issues. Foster's engaged a psychologist to monitor some of the expatriates' behavioural changes or psychological difficulties. He was on 24-hour call by phone for three years. The HR manager and the psychologist also visited all three brewery sites three times a year. During one of the visits to Shanghai an expatriates joked, 'He is back to see if we have gone mad.' The psychologist replied, 'I know you are mad, I just want to see how mad you are.'

The situation today in China is different if positions are located in Shanghai, Beijing or other major cities. These cities are often more advanced than some in Western countries. Availability and variety of Western food is vast and free cable channels are widely available in many different languages. However, if the assignments are in more remote cities, the situation would be different.

It was accepted by most expatriates at Foster's that they were well looked after financially, had generally good accommodation and they were entitled to R&R (rest and recreation) every six months. Several talked about R&R being the only motivating factor that kept them sane. The changing environment of China and its rapid economic development has been so great that no Western companies now provide R&R as part of the employment package as expatriates can find a wide range of entertainment and recreational activities in China. In short, China is no longer considered a 'hard place' to live.

In 1993 and 1994, accommodation comparable to Western standard was not widely available in China. The first group of expatriates at Foster's did lots of house hunting to find something suitable. Green Valley was the first block of Western-style apartments in Shanghai designed purposely for expatriates. It was a long way out of town so required several hours of travelling every day. It was the only expatriate accommodation available at the time; expatriates with families could not live in closer hotels because facilities were not suitable for family life with children.

This meant that each working day was, on average, 12 to 14 hours including travelling time. The situation is different today and expatriates rarely live in hotels for long periods. Other suitable accommodation is available and companies pay less to compensate for accommodation costs.

None of these would be issues that managers in Australia would need to deal with. But for expatriates in China without prior knowledge or training, dealing with these matters was difficult and frustrating. In Shanghai, the general manager had to find houses, pay children's school fees and cope with expatriates who were depressed for one reason or another. He also had to deal with depressed and angry wives.

The need to generate motivation was much greater than in Australia. Of course, the managers themselves were under extreme pressure and it was increasingly difficult for them to perform their duties and function efficiently. The point is, an expatriate position in China has many additional dimensions of complications. Therefore it is essential that organisations have support systems and procedures that will compensate for these complications and take them into account for expatriates' performance.

When duties include love songs

Cross-cultural management positions were vastly different from normal management positions. On top of a normal general manager's duties there were others that were specifically related to culture. The general managers at Shanghai Foster's found themselves being responsible for achieving blood donation quotas and ensuring birth control rates were kept within government regulations and policies. All Chinese organisations had a responsibility to ensure an annual blood donation quota was filled. They were set on a voluntary basis in theory but in reality it was compulsory. Birth control quotas to be met by organisations were set by the relevant government body.

General managers probably would not have understood why these tasks were part of their job. Clearly, multiple approaches are required to deal with multiple cultures, and studies show that those who are skilled in mono-cultural management rarely succeed in multicultural or bicultural environments (Littrell 2002).

Expatriate managers were required to frequently appear in public for all types of public relations purposes, such as sales and marketing, regardless of their actual company role. 'We just had to appear because we were the only foreigners,' one manager commented. These activities once extended to singing love songs in Chinese on a Shanghai radio station.

The critical point of this issue of extra duties, either mundane or serious, as in the one-child policy, was that unless general managers were trained (that is, were mainland Chinese expatriates with previous specific experience) they were not prepared for them and were likely to suffer from culture shock. Nor would they have strategies to deal with such matters, adding to their frustration and further affecting their performance and productivity.

Another key point of cultural difference in managing Chinese joint ventures was the constant discussions and negotiations related to the agreement, which would normally not be matters needing senior management attention. For instance, at Foster's there was the memorable '22 families' issue and the huge volume of documents written back and forth discussing it: the retraction from the original contract, changing the contract conditions, and the gradual drip of information rather than being upfront.

Twenty-two families lived within the compound of Huaguang Brewery. It was agreed initially during negotiations that the joint venture would pay for their relocation. The cost was initially put at around 1.6 million renminbi but was later increased to 5.6 million renminbi. It appeared that each time a figure was agreed upon, an additional factor would be brought up and additional costs were found.

'Approval' is part of a continuing process

The issue highlighted a cultural difference: the ability to see changes as part of a process rather than a retraction of conditions. The learning process is highlighted in a note written by one of the Australian leaders in the joint venture process: 'Troy advises that the Shanghai Foreign Investment Commission has formally approved the joint venture. Now I understand it requires the approval of a multitude of authorities.'

In theory, this meant that if any link in the chain of government bodies did not approve, there would be no joint venture. Many communication notes in October 1993 discussed the timing and likelihood of obtaining a licence. At first the Australians thought it was just a matter of process and procedure. After five months of processing, one wrote: 'I am still led to believe the licence should not be a problem.'

In comparison, setting up a business is relatively easy in Australia or other Western cultures. Engaging an accountant or lawyer to set up a company is straightforward. In China, approval at different levels of government is required and these requirements can differ from province to province, city to city. The complexity of obtaining a business operating licence is unique and expatriate managers cannot be prepared for it. The only effective management solution is for them to have an adaptable attitude and go along with whatever is required of them.

The general manager of Shanghai in 1993 recalled the day they obtained their business operation licence.

> On the morning of 15 November 1993, Stewart Luk came into the office with his briefcase and solemnly said, 'Let's go'. I thought he meant negotiations had fallen through and we were leaving Shanghai. Then he said, 'Let's go and get a business licence!' Stewart has a great sense of theatre. It was the day of Foster's entry into China, a historical moment for Foster's after more than two years of negotiations.

Financial management, an area of great importance for any organisation, was also subject to cultural differences. The Shanghai joint venture started without the support of any working capital. It was rationalised that Guangming was a profitable operation before the joint venture and therefore the operating capital could be supported by cash sales.

This did not happen. For about 18 months, Shanghai struggled to the point where 'the joint venture is now living out of the pockets of the six expatriates'. There were notes that mentioned moving into a new office, but there were 'no funds to buy any filing cabinets, desks, etc (trying to chase up some furniture around the plant)'. On one occasion, it is claimed the general manager and guests were served tea, 'but there were no tea leaves in the cups, just hot water, because there was not enough money to buy any tea'.

This lack of liquidity in the operation took up much of the general manager's and deputy general manager's time, increasing frustration dramatically and certainly affecting productivity in general.

'Unforeseen matters', an appropriate term, were another cultural barrier. These were matters that the Chinese saw as normal but were unforeseen by the Australians. Local staff salary structures and canteen complaints were foreign to expatriate managers. The base salary was less than $50 a month. Additional items, including heating fees in winter, hygiene fees to compensate for poor bathing facilities, and more than 20 other items, added up to almost $250 a month per person. Understanding and orchestrating such complex packages was indeed a challenge.

Organisations need to understand that expatriates in China work under extreme circumstances because of China's unique system and structure. It is also suggested that the measurement of success of the operation should use a range of criteria rather than financial measures only. In addition, much more time should be allowed for managers to perform.

References

Blackman, C., 1995, *Australian Executives in China: The Management Challenge* (Australia China Chamber of Commerce and Industry, Melbourne).

Copeland, M., 1987, 'International training', in R. L. Craig ed, *Training and Development Handbook* (McGraw-Hill, New York).

Davidson, P., and R. W. Griffin, 2003, *Management, An Australian Perspective* (Wiley, Queensland).

Kaye, M., and W. G. Taylor, 1997, Expatriate culture shock in China: a study in the Beijing hotel industry, *Journal of Management Psychology* 12, 496–510.

Lawson, M., 2002, It's not what you say, *Financial Review Boss*.

Littrell, R. F., 2002, Desirable leadership behaviours of multi-cultural managers in China, *Journal of Management Development* 21, 5–74.

McDonald, H., 2004, Tensions simmer in China's not-so-happy 'family', *The Age*, November 6, p. 22.

Purves, B., 1991, *Barefoot in the Boardroom – Venture and Misadventure in the People's Republic of China* (Allen & Unwin, Sydney).

Selmer, J., 2000, Psychological barriers to international adjustment: North American vs. Western European business expatriates in China, *Cross-cultural Management – An International Journal* 7, 13–18.

8

Cultural obstacles to negotiations: new research in China

Abstract: This chapter utilises research material from a recent cross-cultural negotiation project. The authors aim at identifying a few critical points of characters when negotiating with Chinese.

1. Cultural differences
2. The meaning of Confucian culture and its five formal relationships
3. The impact of Mao on the Chinese culture
4. The important role of Communist party and party secretaries
5. The impact of single child polity on the Chinese culture and the new 4–2–1 family
6. The key to success – bicultural negotiators

Key words: negotiation with Chinese, negotiation styles, cross-cultural negotiation, commercial negotiation with Chinese, Confucian culture, hidden agendas, high and low context culture, Maoism, PR China, Confucianism's five formal relationships, Communist Party, Party secretary, Western business people, harmony, collective culture, 'guanxi', China's education revolution, 4–3–1 family, single child policy, hierarchy, bicultural negotiators, the meaning of 'yes'.

This chapter is the result of collaborative research by Dr Mona Chung and Dr Richard Ingleby, Visiting Professors at North China University of Technology.

A research project was conducted in 2008 in an effort to develop strategies to overcome cultural obstacles in negotiations between Australians and Chinese business people. Its aim was to highlight the uniqueness of Chinese culture, which has not been clearly identified in past research, especially the importance of the Cultural Revolution on Chinese contemporary culture. The research provides valuable insights into how and why this unique Chinese culture exists.

Understanding different approaches

It is accepted that Australians and Chinese have different approaches to negotiation, and Australian companies and government bodies encounter problems in negotiating with the Chinese. Attempts to improve cross-cultural communication are hampered by incomplete knowledge of the reasons for, and implications of, the differences. The overall strategies of our project were to:

1. Reduce the possibilities for misunderstanding by developing more sophisticated understandings of Australian and Chinese negotiation and communication strategies and styles.

2. Devise and test strategies to improve cross-cultural communication.

The importance of the project was more than theoretical. The isolated nature of Chinese society between 1949 and 1979 means there are few Australian businesses that have longstanding relationships or experiences with their Chinese counterparts. Australian businesses have only dealt with mainland China, the People's Republic of China (PRC), since the 'open-door' policy began in 1979 (Png 1992). From 1949 to 1979 the PRC had very limited trade with the international community and there was also very little cultural and information exchange (Schauble 2001).

Since 1979 there has been very rapid development of both industrialisation and trade in China. The Chinese have effectively undergone their Industrial Revolution four or five times faster than Western countries did in the eighteenth and nineteenth centuries. The speed of Chinese modernisation has correlated with an increase in the importance of China to Australia, as clearly shown in rapidly increasing trade figures. Since 2007 China has been Australia's largest trading partner.

Culture and its impact on negotiation

This project was obviously part of a more general increase in China business research. A speaker (Bush 2008) at a 2008 conference, whose justifying theme was that 'China is still disconnected from the West by confusing and complex cultural exchanges', suggested the aim of research should: (1) be historically accurate; (2) bring to light things that are unknown; and (3) understand better those things that currently seem insufficiently understood or appreciated.

The authors of this chapter contend that cross-cultural negotiation between the West and China is 'insufficiently understood' rather than 'unknown' because it has been the subject of previous research. Existing studies of the negotiation process between the West and China have established that there are differences between the way the two different cultures communicate intra-culturally (Adler, Braham, and Graham 1992); and such insights have led to examination of what happens when the different cultures attempt to communicate with each other (Lee, Yang, and Graham 2006a; Adler, Braham, and Graham 1992).

These studies, based on simulated negotiations and/or interviews and questionnaires (Lee, Yang, and Graham 2006) have attempted to analyse behaviour in terms of cultural characteristics from a variety of disciplinary perspectives, including linguistics (George, Jones, and Gonzalez 1998); psychology (Triandis 1996; Ulijin et al. 2005); and the more general field of business negotiation (Adler and Graham 1989; Fisher, Ury, and Patton 1991; Pye 1982).

One of the most important findings of these studies relates to the importance of Confucian culture, which is shared by people in the PRC and other Chinese nationalities, is the distinctive nature of Confucian culture, which constitutes an entire philosophy of life, makes China more different (vis-à-vis Australia) than the other post-Communist examples arising out of the disintegration of the Soviet empire. Typically, existing studies focus on Confucian concepts, discussed further below, such as harmony, collectivism, face, guanxi and hierarchy.

In terms of Hall's (1976) continuum of high and low context cultures, China is a very high context culture. In low context culture, the speaker uses the minimum level of words and every word used has a specific meaning. Low context Australians use a small number of words to provide a high level of content, whereas high context Chinese people use a large number of words but they have a low level of content.

In high context culture the meanings a communicator seeks to convey come not only from the many more words used, but also from the impressions created by a large amount of background information. Both parties expect meanings will be derived from reading between the lines, which means they are required to understand the entire context.

It's not just what is said, but how

The differences between high and low context cultures extend beyond the number of words used, to the ways in which they are used. High context people organise their information in a different order to low context people (Hall and Hall 1990). In terms of logical order of presenting information, high context people present their evidence first and build up to their conclusion at the end by the accumulation of the evidence and implications arising from it (Chung 2008). Because of this the listener may misunderstand the evidence presented as the final argument or vice versa.

In contrast, low context culture people present their conclusion first and then the evidence to support it (Chung 2008). This way the argument is strong and the purpose of the evidence is clear. In presenting evidence, precise words are used for exact meanings in supporting the argument.

The different ways that information is presented create two major problems in cross-cultural negotiation processes:

1. High context people will not be expecting the argument to be at the start of the discussion and low context people will wonder why high context people never get to the point.

2. Low context people will not look for the implied meanings and messages that high context people seek

to convey in the negotiation process, because they will only be looking for the exact meaning in the words used. High context people will be looking for meanings between the lines and implications that are not actually there.

These phenomena have led to the conclusion that Western business people will not succeed in negotiations with Chinese unless they have Chinese members on their negotiation team (Graham and Lam 2003; Chung 2008).

In this chapter we argue that in interactions involving a high context culture, because so much of the meaning accorded to interactions is part of the context, researchers may fall into the trap of thinking they understand behaviour by being able to report recognised patterns of communication. In high context culture in particular, an interactional phenomenological approach to research is required. Failure to do so creates the danger of the 'Glass Wall' effect (Chung 2008), whereby outsiders think they understand a phenomenon because they can describe it, but are unable to properly explain the phenomenon because they do not understand the totality of the background.

The literature in explaining Chinese culture and culturally influenced behaviours has so far focused on Confucianism alone, which is not enough to explain the behaviour of mainland Chinese. The distinctive feature of mainland Chinese culture vis-à-vis the rest of the world is created by the unique combination of Confucianism and Maoism.

There is a crucial difference between mainland China (PRC) and overseas Chinese groups (Chung and Smith 2007). The 'cultural difference' label is not sufficient to describe the political difference deriving from the fact that mainland China has had a particular, and extreme, history since 1949. There are differences – caused by the variable of

Maoism and in particular the Cultural Revolution – between mainland Chinese on the one hand, and people from 'Chinese backgrounds' on the other.

The specific reference to the PRC, as distinct from other ethnic Chinese groups and countries such as Taiwan, Hong Kong, Macau, Singapore and other overseas Chinese communities in, for example, Malaysia, Indonesia, Australia and the United States, is based on the historical significance of Maoism and in particular the Cultural Revolution.

Although this point is acknowledged in passing by one of the existing studies in which a different 'individualism' grading was attributed to Taiwanese research participants as opposed to mainland Chinese, generally speaking (existing studies' exceptions being use of the term Chinese to refer to anyone who is a member of a group), that is part of the broader Chinese culture (Lee, Yang, and Graham 2006b).

The importance of Maoism

A full understanding of the implications of this crucial difference is required if Australians, and Western people more generally, are to have a sufficient understanding of China in order to negotiate successfully with the Chinese. We do not say that the existing discussion of Confucianism is irrelevant; rather that the focus needs to be on the relationship between Confucianism and Maoism. Generally speaking, the exist ing literature about China stresses the importance of Confucianism but is relatively silent about the importance of Maoism.

The first importance of Maoism is in terms of the influence of the Communist Party on all aspects of life, including the relationship between political influence and career advancement. Western society is characterised by separation of powers on many levels. Although there are obvious questions as to the extent to which the ideal is matched in practice, there is in liberal Western democracies at least the need to maintain a distinction between legislature, executive and judiciary.

Further, in many liberal Western democracies there is a diffusion of political power affected by federalism (whether internal as in Australia, or external as in the European Union). Also, the democratic process in liberal Western democracies is characterised by changes in the extent to which the legislature is controlled by particular political groupings.

In China the legislature, executive and judiciary are all controlled by the Communist Party and the party is the only effective political grouping. This has been the case for all practical purposes since 1949, so there are few people in China with any living memory of anything else.

The second importance of Maoism is the impact of the Cultural Revolution on Confucian culture. This is a 'high trust' culture, where people's interactions are based on the expectations generated by relationships and hierarchies, in contrast with the more 'deal-based' assumptions of individualist liberal society. But one of the effects of the Cultural Revolution was to challenge the assumption that personal relationships provided security. The imposition of political will transcended family and other relationships, and created a situation where no individual could treat another without suspicion that the interaction might be used to their disadvantage for political purposes.

The Chinese do not discuss the Cultural Revolution easily, although there are few families who can have escaped experience of it from one side or another. The experience of the Cultural Revolution is not part of mainstream primary and secondary education, and the official Government policy can only be interpreted as an attempt to ignore a bad memory, analogously perhaps to the Vichy French collaboration with the Nazis. The following sections of the chapter look at the relationship between key Confucian concepts and Maoism.

Confucianism's five formal relationships

It is an acknowledged feature of Confucian philosophy that every person has a specified role in the collective culture. The gradation from continuum of 'individual to collective' is one of the dimensions used by Hofstede (2001) in his framework of variables to conduct cross-cultural studies. Confucian philosophy conceptualises society as a collective organisation of hierarchies based on five sets of formal relationships, each with specific obligations and responsibilities, and on the basis of which all other relationships are modelled (Chan 2003). These are: 1. Man and the state; 2. Man and his wife; 3. Man and his siblings; 4. Man and his children; 5. Man and his father.

The acceptance of these hierarchical relationships creates an acceptance that there are differentials of power and status, another of Hofstede's variables being 'power distance'. This means that individuals define themselves in relation to each other by reference to the differences in power (in relation to Japan see Brett and Okumura (1998) and more generally see Hofstede 2001)) of Hall's (1990) low context to high context continuum, discussed with particular application to business negotiation by Graham, Mintu and Rodgers (1994) and Mintu-Wimsatt and Gassenheimer (2000). In high context cultures such as the Chinese, people are deeply involved in embedded relationships with each other.

In Maoist (as in Leninist) political philosophy, the party is paramount. The collective nature of Chinese culture, and the antipathetic approach to public dissent, makes it less likely there will be public opposition to the paramount status of the party. The importance the Communist Party attaches to party discipline is consistent with the Confucian concepts of five specified relationships.

For example, in the authors' interactions with the Law School at Beijing University One, we attended meetings with the Dean, the Research Director and the Party Secretary. Their real roles were only revealed to us because one of our team members was of mainland Chinese origin, an insider (Chung, 2008). When the Dean took us to dinner, the Party Secretary or his deputy was always present. It is inconceivable that a faculty in an Australian university would have its own party secretary.

The predominance of the Communist Party in Chinese organisations has yet to be acknowledged in the literature. It is a feature that cannot be derived from interviews or questionnaires, from studies of people of Chinese background rather than from the PRC, or from research which physically does not take place in China. But Western business people need to be in China and know what happens there if they are to do business there.

The collective nature of Chinese culture (Hofstede 2001) also means that negotiations are typically conducted by teams, and often they do not have the authority to conclude a deal because approval needs to come from elsewhere (Chung 2008; Beamer 1998). The approval may include that of the Communist Party. It can be difficult for Australians, who are imbued in an individualistic culture where each person in a commercial entity has specific powers and duties, to actually know who holds the power across the other side of the table. It can also be frustrating for many days of negotiation to be concluded with the statement, 'We'll get back to you.'

The need to maintain harmony within and between the hierarchies created by the Confucian philosophy of five sets of relationships means that all members of society are obliged to maintain the balance between these hierarchies (Chung 2008; Graham and Lam 2003). The acceptance of and need to maintain harmony means there is an aversion to open displays of conflict. The concepts of face and harmony are related to high context communication, because implicit understandings are slowly built up and the possibilities of rejection and conflict minimised (Chung 2008). The Confucian concept of face requires individuals to maintain self-respect and to respect other members of society, to maintain a harmonious society (Kirkbride, Tang, and Westwood 1991).

When 'normal' behaviour is 'aggressive'

This contrasts with Western society, where open disagreement between business people is not necessarily frowned upon and may even be seen as an indicator of a healthy 'open' relationship. One consequence is that 'normal' Western behaviour may be seen as inappropriately aggressive by the Chinese (Lee, Yang, and Graham 2006a). Another is that the two cultures have entirely different approaches to the use of legal remedies (Shenkar and Ronen 1987).

The 'bargaining in the shadow of the law' and 'litigotiation' frameworks that have dominated Western socio-legal studies of negotiation for nearly 30 years, could not be used in relation to Chinese society without adaptation. Western business people, generally, focus on the 'deal' and content of the outcome, most typically by resolving areas of disagreement one by one and with signed contracts representing the closure of a deal and the framework that will govern the future relationship between the parties.

For the Chinese, the focus is on progressing the intensity of the relationship. The relationship governs the terms of the contract and also its implementation. This means that from the Chinese perspective, the terms of the document are not a final determination of the parties' rights and responsibilities vis-à-vis each other.

This is all clearly related to 'guanxi', a concept so distinctively Confucian that there is no suitable English translation (Chung 2006; Graham and Lam 2003: 86; Kirkbride, Tang, and Westwood 1991). Guanxi is a relationship built on a practised form of respect and obligation that adheres to Confucian hierarchical values, where favours are given and received only when there is mutual benefit involved (however, not necessarily in any particular sequential order) and in accordance with how people conduct themselves.

Guanxi is very different from the concept of contract, or more colloquially 'the deal', which is the basis of Western commercial transactions. But the understandings on this level have not been sufficient to enable Western businesses to deal easily with their Chinese counterparts.

The importance of guanxi is linked to the concepts of insider and outsider. Chinese gravitate towards each other especially when there are outgroup members. They will trust their fellow Chinese first if they are faced with insiders and outsiders. Certain things may be said to other Chinese that will never be said to Western outsiders.

This phenomenon derives from the importance of face in a high-trust culture, and the implication is the value to Western negotiation teams of having a Chinese member

(Graham and Lam 2003; Kirkbride, Tang, and Westwood 1991; Chung 2008). The second reason for the mistrust of foreigners is that the Chinese have been invaded by both Japan and Western powers, and have a perception of being exploited by European colonialism.

Negotiation with Chinese in practice

Our research project examined communication between Australian and mainland Chinese from a commercial perspective by a cross-cultural team, in order to develop and test strategies to overcome impediments to successful Australian–Chinese negotiation. We argue that an understanding of cross-cultural negotiation requires analysis of the reasons for the culturally specific differences between Australians and Chinese, rather than observations of the effect of those differences alone.

This is necessary not only to clarify the theoretical assumptions underlying the project but also because many Australian and Chinese business people are unaware of the existence and importance of such differences. In addition, a full understanding of the dynamics of cross-cultural negotiation requires qualitative methods such as participant observation and simulation.

It is only by analysing the content of interactions that we can develop problem-solving strategies. Quantitative methods are less well-suited for the analysis of the phenomenon because human behaviours in communication process are ephemeral and unique (Chung and Smith 2008). In addition, there are specific cultural biases which derive that flow from researchers and respondents to interviews and questionnaires having culturally based assumptions in relation to questions and answers. In particular, Chinese respondents to Likert Scale inquiries will cluster around the midrange, because the desire for harmony means the extreme options will be disregarded.

Simulation is a common qualitative method in this area because cross-cultural negotiation is not easily accessible for participant observation. Because of the preference for quantitative studies in the American academy, simulations are primarily used to generate quantitative data. The reliability of this data depends on the extent to which the application of the quantitative variables can escape the cultural assumptions of the researchers and research assistants.

As part of an exploratory pilot study, we:

- Organised commercial negotiation simulations between Australians and Chinese and Chinese–Chinese negotiation teams at Beijing University One and Beijing University Two.
- Conducted some 'negotiation games' with undergraduate students at Beijing University One and Beijing University Three.

These were universities where we had connections of a personal and professional nature. At Beijing University One, where one of the authors has a family connection, we had been responsible for conducting discussions about institutional collaborations and had each given guest lectures, the reason we were each appointed Visiting Professors. At Beijing University Two there was a particular collaborative relationship with an academic involving joint publication. Beijing University Three had a pre-existing relationship with our home institutions because of undergraduate student enrolments.

We specifically organised the Chinese–Chinese negotiation teams to conduct negotiation simulations of the same scenario in both English and Chinese, so that we could consider the language variable. Each negotiation team was given a set of common facts and a specific briefing in relation to their role that was not made available to the other team. The Australian–Chinese negotiation simulations were in relation to the same scenarios but were only conducted in English. The simulations (which were recorded digitally) were observed by a team of Australian Chinese researchers.

The negotiation games (which are far less sophisticated than those previously recorded (Adler and Graham 1989) were first devised 'on the run' at Beijing University Three to illustrate points made in a lecture on cross-cultural negotiation. Students were paired and assigned the role of buyer and seller. They were told that: they had 60 seconds to negotiate the price of 1 kilogram of rice; any pair that did not reach agreement would be eliminated; the three purchasers who paid the most would be eliminated; and the three vendors who obtained the lowest price would be eliminated.

The prices each pair arrived at were all displayed on the board and then there were successive rounds until a winning buyer and a winning seller were decided.

Be prepared – the future of Chinese negotiators

One of the first challenges in devising a research project based on simulation is to find suitable participants. We took advantage of our pre-existing relationship with Beijing University One to propose simulated negotiations between academics from that university and members of a delegation from our own university.

In the week before the delegation's visit we had two preparatory interactions with our Chinese colleagues. In the first, we were invited to provide feedback to an international trade simulation, conducted in English, by a group of commerce students. We were applauded by the students and our colleagues responded to our feedback to the students in extremely complimentary terms.

This in itself might seem something positive, but events were to show that the reasons for the response included the seeds of the problem of why the pilot did not proceed as anticipated.

In the second interaction, we wanted a simulation of a Chinese–Chinese negotiation, but our requirement that this be in English meant that not all our Chinese colleagues felt able to participate. Their attitude probably derived in part from their desire not to lose face by 'losing the simulation' in front of their students and their colleagues. Both colleagues and students prepared for the simulations by explicitly talking about what they had to do to 'win', an approach that contrasts with the 'win-win' philosophy emphasised in their teaching materials.

Our colleagues at Beijing University One informed the Chinese observer that they were reluctant to be used as guinea pigs, and were also concerned that their performance in the simulation might be used as part of their peer evaluation. Not all of this attitude can be ascribed to the novelty of simulation because it is clear that simulation is an integral part of the curriculum.

However, the use of simulation as a research method might be less accepted in the Chinese context; and the surveillance nature and history of mainland China means that participants may be reluctant to expose themselves in this manner. It is important to observe that the Chinese participants' reluctance was communicated only in private and only to the Chinese observer, who had insider status. A research team that did not include an insider would not have received this information.

China's education revolution

By contrast, the students were initially only too enthusiastic to participate. One possible explanation for this is that the students have had a different educational experience from that of their lecturers. In addition to the recent Chinese Industrial Revolution, there has also been an education revolution.

Universities were actually closed down during the Cultural Revolution. But today a far greater proportion of China's gross domestic product goes into education than is the case in Western countries, and one of the focuses of contemporary Chinese education is a hunger for international knowledge and experience. This is shown by the fact that many classes are taught in English, English is a compulsory feature of the final-year school examination, and there are specific courses on negotiation with Western business people.

Although the students were initially enthusiastic, their response to being given scenarios was to ask where they could find the precedent for their response and at the end of the first simulation they asked the Western observer what the 'right answer' was to the problem. They were visibly upset at the response that there was no 'right answer' to this or to most negotiation problems. Chinese education differs from Australian in that in China there is a far greater emphasis on rote learning and much less emphasis on active learning methods.

During the simulation between the students we observed, they were reading from prepared texts. Although this might, in part, have been because of language difficulties, it remained the case that the simulated negotiation was an exchange of positions in the bargaining sense rather than any attempt to engineer compromise based on common interest in the more committed sense of negotiation (Adler, Braham, and Graham 1992).

It was clear that the undergraduate students lacked the commercial and life experience necessary to conduct simulation of even straightforward transactions, which was one of the reasons for conducting the 'price of rice' game. It was often observed by the research team that statements straight from text books were read out in negotiation simulations. In some cases, the entire section of a text book was read out.

The limitation was also observed at their inability to move forward on one topic. It often resulted in a 'ping-pong' game instead of negotiating around issues and moving forward. This conclusion was reinforced by the final simulation, in which postgraduate commerce students participated on a far more sophisticated level of interaction.

Another distinguishing feature of Chinese education is its highly competitive and ranked nature. Many students were visibly upset by their exclusion in the negotiation game (at both universities where this game was played). One interesting exception to the competitive nature of the students was the observed behaviour in the 'price of rice' game at Beijing University Three. Some of the 'losing' participants were initially reluctant to leave the game and only did so when isolated by counting the number of tables remaining. The bargaining pairs consulted with each other to try to reach agreed prices, which kept them in the game by not excluding buyers who paid too much or sellers who got too little. There was no evidence of this at Beijing University One.

The competitive nature of the undergraduate students sits uneasily with the Confucian desire for harmony but is explainable in terms of:

1. The extremely competitive nature of the Chinese education system, where students and their schools and universities are ranked for competitive entry from the stage of kindergarten.

2. The egocentric nature of the products of the single-child policy although this comment is perhaps more tentative. Almost all Chinese aged 18 to 21 are not only single children, but also children of single children, leading to the nicknames of 'Little Emperors/Empresses' and '4-2-1' children; that is each child has the undivided attention of two parents and four grandparents. It was striking that one of the most frequent statements in negotiation was simply 'I want' – a point to which we will return when commenting on the applicability of the frameworks for analysis introduced by Adler, Braham, and Graham (1992) and Adair, Okumura, and Brett (2001) in relation to Japan.

An important implication of the above is that the successful conduct of simulations will require graduate students or executive trainees, so that participants have sufficient skills and life experience to negotiate in a commercial sense; and that each party to the negotiation should be of equal status. This obviously presents a challenge in terms of arranging for Australians and Chinese to be in the same place at the same time. Lee, Yang and Graham (2006b) used American MBA students on an international course in Hong Kong.

The negotiation topic was also important. It was observed that in the first attempt by the Chinese students to negotiate a complex technical commercial contract, little negotiation was conducted as they were pushed by time. Therefore when time was limited, future negotiations were designed to be simple in term of facts.

Is English a true global language?

The question of language remains a difficult one. It was absolutely striking at Beijing Universities One and Two that the simulations conducted in English were categorised by more aggressive behaviour, body language and raised voices. An Australian colleague who observed the simulations at Beijing University Two commented that the female participants were silent in the Chinese language phase and prominent in the English version.

On one level the use of English as the language for simulations can be justified in terms of it being the language that will invariably be used in single-language negotiations. But the limits of the English language as a negotiation tool for Western negotiators are one of the reasons Western negotiation teams are unlikely to be successful in China without a Chinese member of the team (Graham and Lam 2003; Chung 2008).

Hierarchy and harmony – two key cultural features

The difficulties which qualitative researchers typically endure in the location of willing participants are accentuated in a society where a single political party controls every aspect of an individual's life. Although there are occasions when academic freedom is honoured more in the breach than in the observance, it remains the case that Western academics generally conduct their research without fear of being adversely judged by their colleagues. In Western societies, university researchers can often take advantage of the independent and non-threatening nature of their institutions to secure access to data.

In Australia there is a difference between 'I'm from the University and I'd like to do research', and 'I'm from the Tax Office and I'd like to do research'. Features of Western academic life do not apply to the same extent in China because the requisite levels of trust do not exist. Similarly, Western academics seeking to research Chinese culture (even as part of cross-cultural studies) need to overcome suspicion of the outsider, which is part of contemporary Chinese culture.

In relation to negotiation as an area of cross-cultural study, the classic frameworks of Western socio-legal study are typified by Mnookin and Kornhauser (1979) 'Bargaining in the shadow of the law' and Galanter's (1984) concept of 'litigotiation' to illustrate the strategic and simultaneous use of litigation and negotiation. But in China the legal system is far less established in a historical sense, and the absence of transparency in the Western sense means the system lacks even the generalised guidance of common law principles. The relevance of legal rights and remedies is also lessened by the importance attached to relationships as a source of obligation.

If Western observers are to properly analyse Chinese behaviour in negotiations, their frameworks will need to account for the more diffuse nature of decision-making in Chinese negotiation teams.

The combination of the collective (Hofstede 2001) and hierarchical features of Chinese culture means that many responses in negotiation relate to the internal requirements of the negotiation team (Chung 2008; Graham and Lam 2003). This can be confusing for Australian negotiators who may be looking for a 'hard' and 'soft' approach when this is not the explanation for the behaviour.

Even in a ceremony to appoint the authors of this chapter as Visiting Professors, the Dean ensured that all members of the university spoke in response to the appointments.

However, the final decision is made by the person of highest status but is presented and perceived as a team decision.

The respect for hierarchy and harmony might create a reluctance to participate in experimental research, which puts the reputation of the academic at risk unless the research is actively supported by senior academics within the institution, such as Deans and/or Presidents. Junior academics in China are more accepting of the concept that they can be directed to participate in particular research projects, than are Australians.

The mention of harmony in negotiations by Chinese negotiators is frequent, especially when it appears that conflict is about to occur.

Chinese negotiators – the key to success

The prominence of relationships as a source of obligation means that a full understanding of the dynamics of negotiation will require analysis of interactions between the same groups of people over a period of time.

The techniques used to code negotiation behaviours in previous studies are not sufficiently sophisticated to enable an understanding of the dynamics of cross-cultural negotiation. They are typically influenced and scoped by Western researchers that simply do not reflect Chinese negotiation behaviours. The techniques are generally drawn from typical low context statements that derive their meaning from the words used. High context negotiation behaviour does not fit within these behavioural patterns.

To understand the Chinese negotiation behaviours it is necessary to have Chinese members of a cross-cultural research team, so the questions and observations contain an understanding of both cultures as well as the language aspects.

In this pilot study the high context negotiators often attempted to become more involved with their counterparts by directing discussions towards topics outside the negotiation items. Their statements often started as something that will not create conflict, 'Have another drink, have some more duck . . .' They also used far more words, although the words used did not explicitly refer to the subject matter of the negotiation.

'Yes' does not always mean 'yes'

There is a precise difference between Chinese and Australians in relation to the use of the word 'yes' (and as a consequence the use of the word 'no'). In Chinese there is no generalised use of the single word 'yes', as in English. Two different Chinese words translate to 'yes' in English: one confirms a statement has been made; another confirms the statement is true.

The likelihood that the first meaning is intended is increased by the previously discussed phenomenon of Chinese people not wanting to lose face by admitting to a lack of knowledge or understanding. Problems can be caused by the fact that Australians treat the absence of explicit disagreement as agreement (Beamer 1998). There are at least five meanings expressed in the word 'yes' by a Chinese speaker:

1. 'I heard the sound you just made.'
2. 'I am still here.'
3. 'I can't say no because that is too rude. I will say yes so you don't lose face.'

4. 'To keep harmony I will say yes. I will work out later what I will do.'

5. 'I agree with you. I will do this. I agree to comply.'

Australians are used to dealing with binary 'yes/no' alternatives, whereas high context Chinese culture looks more at graduated 'how much' alternatives.

'Yes' was frequently used by the high context negotiators but with the appearance to the Australians of being at random. At one point a team of five participants had three saying 'yes' and two saying 'no' to the same question. When the Australian colleague specifically questioned each participant for the meaning of their particular 'yes' or 'no', the Chinese team members gave answers avoiding a direct 'yes' or 'no'. Instead they were offering explanations of why they said 'yes' or 'no'.

Negotiation with Chinese is a complex task

One conclusion of the preliminary study is that the design of the research is itself constrained by the cultural, political and communication factors that influence the phenomenon constituting the subject matter of the research (Adler and Graham 1989). The centrality of trust to the formation of relationships, combined with the absence of trust resulting from the Cultural Revolution and the omnipresence of the Communist Party, puts 'outsiders' in a difficult position.

It took three visits of approximately ten days each, over a period of about 14 months, for the authors of this chapter to develop a strong relationship with Beijing University One, even though one of the authors already had 'insider' status through her father being a retired professor there. Even with these personal links, it remains the case that the institution is an institution and that collaboration requires the trust of individual people.

It seems clear that participants for simulations will come from the ranks of students, and that graduate students will be required to enable the necessary level of life and commercial experience to be brought to the simulation.

The questions that we seek to explore in further study concern whether it is possible, by third-party mediators or cross-cultural intermediaries (Chung 2008), rather than the more diffuse effect of cultural adaptation (Pornpitakpan 1999; Adler and Graham 1989), to enable negotiations to proceed more freely when parties can have the other's behaviours and responses (as discussed in Adler and Graham (1989) and George, Jones, and Gonzalez (1998)) explained to each other in terms of their cultural specificity.

For example, Australian negotiators might be less likely to view their Chinese negotiation partners as evasive or dishonest if they understood the particular techniques used to express negatives (Lee, Yang, and Graham 2006a; Gilsdorf 1997); and as obsequious if they understood that flattery is a form of politeness.

Similarly, Chinese negotiators might be less likely to view their Australian negotiation partners as rude if they state their positions explicitly and without ambiguity; and stupid if they actually express the contents of the desired outcome at all.

References

Adair, W. L., T. Okumura, and J. M. Brett, 2001, Negotation behavior when cultures collide: The United

States and Japan, *Journal of Applied Psychology* 86, 371–385.

Adler, N. J., R. Braham, and J. L. Graham, 1992, Strategy implementation: A comparison of face-to-face negotiations in the People's Republic of China and the United States, *Strategic Management Journal* 13, 449–466.

Adler, N. J., and J. L. Graham, 1989, Cross-cultural interaction: The international comparison fallacy?, *Journal of International Business Studies* fall.

Beamer, L., 1998, Bridging business cultures, *The China Business Review* 25, 54–58.

Brett, J. M., and T. Okumura, 1998, Inter- and intracultural negotiation: U.S. and Japanese negotiators, *Academy of Management Journal* 41, 495–510.

Bush, C., 2008, Translations and Transformations, www. crassh.com.ac.uk/events/169/programme/

Chan, J. L., 2003, *China Streetsmart* (Pearson Prentice Hall, Singapore).

Chung, M., 2006, Tackling the Chinese Market, *Marketing*, 5, 48–49.

——, 2008, *Shanghaied: Why Foster's Could Not Survive China* (Heidelberg Press, Melbourne).

Chung, M., and W. Smith, 2007, Overseas Chinese as expatriate managers in China – is their recruitment a solution to cross-cultural management problems for multinationals operating in China?, *The International Journal of Diversity in Organisations, Communities and Nations*, Volume 7.

Chung, M., and W. Smith, 2008, 'The Dual Technique Model within case study approaches to cross-cultural management research in China', in A. Gupta, ed, *Oxford Business and Economics Conference* (International Journal of Business & Economics, Oxford).

Fisher, R., W. Ury, and B. Patton, 1991, *Getting to Yes* (Pelican Books, New York).

Galanter, M., 1984, Worlds of deals: Using negotiation to teach about legal process, *Journal of Legal Education* 34.

George, J. M., G. R. Jones, and J. A. Gonzalez, 1998, The role of affect in cross-cultural negotiations, *Journal of International Business Studies*, 29, 749–772.

Gilsdorf, J. W., 1997, Metacommunication effects on international business negotiating in China, *Business Communication Quarterly* 60, 20–37.

Graham, J. L., and N. M. Lam, 2003, The Chinese negotiation, *Harvard Business Review*, 82–91.

Graham, J. L., A. T. Mintu, and W. Rodgers, 1994, Explorations of negotiation behaviours in ten foreign cultures using a model developed in the United States, *Management Science* 40, 72–95.

Hall, E. T., 1976, *Beyond Culture* (Anchor Press/Doubleday & Company Inc., New York).

Hall, E. T., 1990, *The Silent Language* (Anchor Press/ Doubleday & Company Inc., New York).

Hall, E. T., and M. R. Hall, 1990, *Understanding Cultural Differences* (Intercultural Press, Inc., Yarmouth, ME).

Hofstede, G., 2001, *Culture's Consequences* (Sage Publications, Thousand Oaks).

Kirkbride, P., S. F. Y. Tang, and R. I. Westwood, 1991, Chinese Conflict preferences and negotiating behaviour: Cultural and psychological influences, *Organization Studies* 12, 365–386.

Lee, K.-h., G. Yang, and J. L. Graham, 2006, Tension and trust in international business negotiations: American executives negotiating with Chinese executives, *Journal of International Business Studies* 37, 623–641.

Mintu-Wimsatt, A., and J. B. Gassenheimer, 2000, The moderating effects of cultural context in buyer–seller negotiation, *Journal of Personal Selling and Sales Management* 20, 1–9.

Mnookin, R., and L. Kornhauser, 1979, Bargaining in the shadow of the law: The case of divorce, *Yale Law Journal* 88, 950–977.

Png, M. L. H., 1992, Equity joint ventures in the People's Republic of China: Problems that continue after more than a decade under the Open Door Policy, *Case Western Reserve Journal of International Law* 24, 589–630.

Pornpitakpan, C., 1999, The effects of cultural adaptation on business relationships: Americans selling to Japanese and Thais, *Journal of International Business Studies* 30, 317–337.

Pye, L. W., 1982, *Chinese Commercial Negotiating Style* (Oelgeschlager Gunn & Hain, Cambridge, MA).

Schauble, J., 2001, A new cultural revolution, with fries, *The Age*, 10 April 2001, p. 11.

Shenkar, O., and S. Ronen, 1987, The cultural context of negotiations: The implications of Chinese interpersonal norms, *Journal of Applied Behavioral Science* 23, 263–275.

Triandis, H. C., 1996, The psychological measurement of cultural syndromes, *American Psychologist* 51, 407–415.

Ulijin, J., A. Rutkowski, R. Kumar, and Y. Zhu, 2005, Patterns of feelings in face-to-face negotiation: A Sino-Dutch pilot study, *Cross Cultural Management* 12, 103–118.

9

Eat, drink and may your business prosper

Abstract: This chapter discusses an important business tool when doing business in China – eating and drinking.

For the first time, eating and drinking are identified as a business strategy and tool rather than unethical behaviour when doing business with Chinese.

By introducing the history of the importance of food, its relationship with the environment and health, it gives readers better understanding of some the etiquette of being at a banquet with Chinese. It also addresses the importance of eating and drinking with Chinese when doing business. It further discusses how food and drinking are related to festivals and therefore how they can be used in building business relationships with Chinese.

Key words: eat, drink, business, rites of eating, the importance of food in China, food and health, food and environment, etiquette of eating and drinking, business strategy, history of eating and drinking, Chinese table manners, chopsticks, eating noise, 'jiu', festivals and eating, banquets, ethics, relationships.

Eating is important in the Chinese culture. There are many phrases that reflect eating. To obtain a job is 'to feed mouths 糊口'; a position is 'a rice bowl 饭碗'; to be employed is '混饭 just to eat'; doing well is 'eat broadly 吃得开 '; being popular is 'eat delicious food 吃香'; being looked after is 'eating a private banquet 吃小灶'; not considering others is 'eat by yourself '; being hurt by others is '(eat) suffer 吃亏'; can't make up one's mind is 'not sure to eat or not 吃不准'; not capable is 'why are you eating? 干什么吃的'; responsibilities beyond capacity is 'if you can't eat it all, you will have to take it with you 吃不了兜着走'; not achieving results is 'eating rice only 吃干饭'.

Rites of eating must be understood

It is important to understand the role of eating and drinking in Chinese culture and business culture in particular. Eating and drinking is used as an effective business tool in China. It flows from the fundamental principles of Chinese food, the harmonious nature of the culture and the philosophy of food, such as its connection with the environment and health. Beyond this fundamental understanding of food and Chinese culture, there are issues of the style of eating and drinking, and social status to consider.

Rites of Chinese eating must be understood because they are fundamental to how to eat at a Chinese banquet, and it is an area that business people often struggle to master. For Chinese festivals and celebrations, food is closely associated with important dates and events. This is essential to understand because banquets associated with festivals are an important business tool.

Case material is provided in this chapter to illustrate how food is used as a business tool. And this chapter also provides a guide to etiquette in eating when doing business.

Important deals can be made during a banquet. Trust can be built at a dinner table, negotiations can be continued at lunch. A banquet can demonstrate the level of hospitality of the host towards the guests, or to display displeasure by not giving the guests enough face, such as by having lower-ranking visitors at the table. Important senior people attending a banquet indicate the importance of a relationship. 'Shanglan' (to grant someone face) could mean that when it comes to business dealings, a smoother path may be expected.

Eating and drinking to the Chinese is a business tool but not a form of bribery, which is how some Westerners see it. It is an opportunity to be social. Food is eaten and shared to demonstrate personal quality.

The Chinese saying 民以食为天 (for people, food is their entire world) suggests eating is the most important activity of people's daily life. Historically, Chinese governments paid great attention to the supply of food to ensure harmonious governance and a peaceful society. A politician from the Chunqiu period (772–481 BC) said 'for emperors, people are their world; for people, food is their world'. Emperors for centuries understood the importance of food for a country to be in peace and harmony. Without sufficient food, there might be riots. In *Zhou Li* (周礼), a book that covers manners and principles during the Zhou period, officers who were in charge of food were all listed in the front of the book to demonstrate the importance of eating.

The environment and health connection

Chinese believe there is a connection between the food we eat and the environment in which we live. In different seasons, different food is used in Chinese cooking to counter changes in the climate. For example, in spring, more acidic food is better, and in summer, bitter-tasting food helps to reduce internal body heat (Simmons 1991).

Chinese believe there is a relationship between food and health because they believe in a harmonious unity of nature and man (Yau 1994). They believe that to eat liver will nourish our liver; to eat brain will nourish our brain; male organs of animals will improve manliness for men. To reach the highest level of Chinese food and eating is harmony, and the principle of this harmony suggests food is directly related to human health (Wang 1981). Well-educated people are taught not to over-eat. Spices should not be used excessively in cooking because over-spiced food will damage our internal organs (Anderson 1997).

The Chinese have yin and yang and the five elements. These are all systems to explain the universe. Yin and yang explains the origin of the universe, and the five elements explain the structure of the universe. In food, there is also yin and yang. In ancient China, meat was considered yang while grain was considered yin (Wan 1994). Therefore meat and grain products must be put in separate containers. When eating there must be a balance of yin and yang, which is some grain and some meat. Farinaceous food (potatoes are not farinaceous in the Chinese cuisine) is always served at the end of a banquet to ensure the harmony (Lafayette De Mente 1994; Ludman and Newman 1984).

Some food has a nature of warmth, some cold. To eat cold-natured food will reduce the internal body heat and warm food usually improves internal heat and provides the body with required energy. A balance of cold and heat is essential for a human body to operate healthily. External factors such as the weather are major elements affecting the body's internal balance. Therefore, using food to adjust balance is an essential health regime for all Chinese (Tan and Wheeler 1988).

In summer, cold drinks such as beer are drunk to cool down the internal heat. In Beijing, mung beans are boiled into broth to stop people from getting heat-stroke. Construction sites, schools and factories provide mung bean drinks to people on hot summer days. Food that is believed to be of a cold nature, such as eggplants, is not recommended for women during their periods. It is believed the coolness of eggplants may damage their health.

Food is also used as an alternative to medicine. Celery and black fungus are used to reduce blood pressure and to clear arteries and veins. Food that is used for health purposes is also developed and changed along with environmental and fashion changes. Stewed pawpaw with silver fungus is served to women at banquets as a beauty therapy.

The concept of food allergy is different in the Chinese perspective. The Chinese term 'jikou' is associated with undesirable food, such as females not eating eggplants during their periods. Although there is proper translation of allergy in Chinese, it is rarely associated with food.

Personally I am allergic to chilli, but I have no way of letting my Chinese friends understand the seriousness of this. It is usually interpreted as 'she does not like chilli, she can't eat much spicy food'. Because the chef also understands 'allergy' as 'she doesn't like chilli', small amounts may still go into dishes and I will be told 'it is not hot'. If I ask my Chinese friends to taste if there is chilli in the food, I would be told 'not much, you can eat it'. For this one thing, when I am in China, I always rely on my Australian colleagues and friends to give a straight answer to the question, is there chilli in the food or not?

Chinese also serve certain food for symbolic reasons. Dumplings are served for New Year because they resemble the shape of money (when money was made from silver). Fish is served for all occasions because 'yu' shares the same pronunciation as 'surplus and wealth'. Mandarin duck, goose and pigeon are symbols of long life, faithfulness, family love and marital fidelity, because these birds mate for life (Swanson 1996).

For similar reasons, family and friends should never cut up one pear and share it because pear phonetically sounds the same as 'fenli (分离)', which means separation, go away, which can all be extended to symbols of death. When visiting patients in hospital, always take apples ('pingguo' 苹果), which sounds the same as 'peace and safe' – appropriate for patients.

Rites and wrongs

Chinese eat together. Usually food is put in the middle and people sit around it. They will talk about the colour and presentation of the food, and discuss the chef's cooking skills. They offer food and drinks to each other rather than eating the portion on their own plates. In this way, Chinese communicate and exchange their thoughts and ideas. It is why Chinese eat at round tables (Civitello 2007; Wang 1993).

Food offering is basic manners when dining with Chinese (Gray 2003). This is different from the Western style of eating where food is divided into small portions, put on individual plates, and individuals eat what is in front of them and do not share.

When eating Chinese food, a certain order should be observed. The most respected people or honourable guests, or the oldest adult, should start first (Cooper 1986). China is a high power distance culture (Hofstede 2001). The higher the position of the honourable guest, the more elaborate the banquet will be. This includes delicacies. It is the duty of a host to show that the guests are properly received. Drinks will reflect this equally, and this will be explained later.

Rites of eating in China are not as simple as manners. They involve protocols, etiquette and ceremonial courtesy (Chance 1992). To eat for hunger is not the primary purpose of attending Chinese banquets. Banquets are for socialising, showing appreciation, building relationships and trust, getting to know someone, politicking and business negotiations.

There is very little in Western literature on how to eat Chinese food. In reality, Westerners often perform poorly at a banquet table, and this is not just referring to whether they can use chopsticks. Worse, some literature even gives incorrect advice on Chinese table manners (Visser 1991), which perhaps was a result of experience with restaurants and/or patrons of a lower standard.

The history of the Chinese culture to discuss matters such as business, policies, etc. at banquets goes back to 22 BC (Xia dynasty) (Lai 1978). In the Zhou dynasty (11 BC), rules and rites were established that were aimed at regulating banquets to eliminate waste. *Zhouli*, *Yili* and *Liji* were the three volumes of writing to record eating and banqueting etiquette.

They covered all the major events such as funerals and festivals, as well as daily eating etiquette. Seating arrangements were recorded. The upper seat (if people sit south–north, then the west seat is the upper seat) was reserved only for the oldest or the most respected person, such as an officer of high position. People stood for the oldest and the most respected when they entered the room. You should always wait for the oldest person to start first and only stop eating when the oldest person finishes (Lafayette De Mente 1994). Eating and drinking was also used as a diplomatic tool in the Chunqiu period. During the year 242 of the Chunqiu period, 450 banquets were recorded.

Chinese also believe that through observing eating, they are able to determine a person's integrity and conduct. This is why a guest is always invited to dine with the host. Those who eat by themselves and never allow others to eat first present poor personal quality. This is the reason a good host must put food into their guest's bowl/plate. They must continue to do this throughout a dinner. The host will continue to say 'please have more' and 'please drink more' throughout the session. This is called 'rangchai (让菜), rangjiu (让酒)'. This is regarded as good basic manners. Those who eat without respect and consideration for others are labelled as 'beasts' by Confucius in his *Book of Rites*.

Similar to Western habits, there are different levels of eating and banqueting in China. Suitable table manners for state banquets are not necessarily required at home or an informal setting. However, in addition to the previously mentioned etiquettes, a few common mistakes Westerners make at Chinese tables are worth mentioning.

Don't wave your chopsticks

The use of chopsticks is important and most Australians are well trained in using them through years of Sunday Yum Cha. Other Westerners vary in terms of their skills. As much as Chinese hosts will keep asking if knives (they often don't have them readily available) and forks are required, you should resist the temptation. Chopsticks are a 3000-year-old tradition, according to the *Book of Rites*. Practice will make mastering the technique easy, usually after a couple of days.

Chopsticks should only be rested on the chopstick pillows provided, not on top of the bowl or plate, not dipped into the bowl of rice, not waved in the air when not eating, and not used as a tool other than putting food to the mouth. Sucking, licking and chewing on chopsticks is simply not acceptable!

The serving dishes must sit in the middle of the table. Restaurants arrange tables to ensure each guest is able to reach every dish. Serving dishes should never be lifted and moved towards yourself, nor should you push food off the serving plates with chopsticks. It is the host's duty to ensure guests will try every dish and have enough food. A good restaurant will ensure all guests are well served and looked after. For guests, it is impolite to finish everything on a serving plate. It implies that the host has not provided enough food.

It is rude at a banquet to make eating noises such as slurping soup. (It may be acceptable in Japan but Japanese culture is not Chinese culture.) Nor should guests make sucking noises, although sound from crunchy vegetables (which is how most vegetables are cooked) is acceptable.

Sharing food with others and giving then the best quality first indicates a person is not selfish or unable to share. This will no doubt reflect other areas of conduct as well. This is demonstrated by good table manners such as putting food in other people's bowls/plates first before serving yourself.

In a Chinese group, the way you handle yourself at the table gives very clear signals as to what kind of a person you are. Good Chinese table manners are the same as good Western table manners and not everyone can master them or know them. Therefore, copying the host or hostess is not an infallible way of learning how to eat Chinese food correctly.

Historically, eating and drinking was used by officials to give subordinates a higher status, especially during time of war. Soldiers were given a good meal with a large quantity of drinks before a major battle. It was also believed that soldiers would be less timid after drinking heavily. Prisoners given death sentences would always be given a good meal with plenty to drink before execution.

Drinking is part and parcel of dining. Alcoholic drinks in Chinese are pronounced 'jiu (酒)', which shares the same pronunciation as 'long time (久)'. So drinking alcohol is symbolic for a long-lasting relationship (Swanson 1996).

Although Chinese do not drink nearly as much wine or beer (Chung 2008) as Westerners, some can drink a large quantity of strong Chinese liquor. The traditional Chinese alcoholic drink is a very strong liquor called 'bai jiu (白酒)', a spirit drunk in small tumblers. Sometimes a competition drinking 'bai jiu' can be a serious game. Chinese hosts must ensure their guests have enough to drink at a banquet. 'Jinxing (尽兴)', to enjoy the moment as much as possible, is the spirit of drinking together.

Drinking is also a way to get to know someone and build a trustworthy relationship. Chinese have a saying, 'the truth reveals after drinks'. So if a guest trusts a host enough to have a good drink with them and not have to worry about 'truth coming out', it indicates the level of trust and honesty of the guest.

The importance of festivals

Chinese do not like odd numbers. Even numbers are considered luckier. But most festivals are on odd-number days, such as January 1 (New Year), May 5 (Duanwu Festival), July 7 (Qixi Festival), August 15 (Moon Festival, the second-largest festival after New Year) and September 9 (Chong Yang Festival). This dislike of odd numbers reflects that these days traditionally were taboo days when people offered food and fruits to ghosts and devils in the hope of keeping them happy, so they would go away.

For each festival, different food is used traditionally. Dumplings are for New Year and moon cakes are for Moon Festival. Most festivals have historical background stories and sometimes there are different versions or even different stories, because they have been told over and over for thousands of years. For example, Qixi Festival is traditionally the equivalent of Valentine's Day.

Some stories are related to historical events and some have been turned into fairytales. Duanwu Festival was to remember the great poet Qu Yuan, who threw himself into the river to demonstrate his loyalty towards his own country. Moon Festival was said to originate from when the Mogos were in control of China. The Han Chinese were planning a riot for August 15. Because they were under strict monitoring by officials and were not allowed meetings, making plans was impossible. So they made moon cakes in which written notes were hidden and delivered.

Hence there is the tradition that moon cakes are given to all friends, relations, acquaintances, associates, clients, and even visitors from afar. Today in business circles, giving clients, customers and associates moon cakes to strengthen the business relationships is common, especially in southern China such as in Guangdong. It is certainly not in any way considered bribery. On the contrary, it is poor form not to give moon cakes, which carries the same meaning as crossing someone off your Christmas list.

A lesson learnt by an Australian company

Eating and drinking is used as a public relations tool to demonstrate status, to show hierarchies, to reward people and staff, to show hospitality, to ensure harmony. All of this is part of the process of building relationships and smoothing business transactions.

Australia's largest beverage company, Foster's Group, established three joint ventures in China from 1993. The first was in Shanghai, with a local partner, Huaguang Brewery. Also in 1993, Guangdong Foster's was established in Doumen, in Guangdong province. In 1995 the joint venture was established in Tianjin. To conduct business successfully, expatriate managers needed to learn the fundamentals of how food was used as a business tool in China.

Huaguang Brewery was part of the Ministry of Light Industry and had all the characteristics of any state-owned Chinese organisation. It had the necessary connections to other government departments, and suppliers and wholesalers. It is fair to suggest that a well-established network was established over the years within the Chinese system.

As part of the operations, banquets and functions were held at times of need; for instance, to secure a good supply contact with a particular contractor would involve a banquet with key people such as the sales manager.

As soon as the joint venture was established, the management team led by Australian expatriate managers decided to stop the practice of banqueting with all suppliers, similar to corporate practice at head office in Australia at the time, to cut costs. Expatriates saw this as part of a Westernisation and modernisation program to introduce 'ethical practice' into the new joint venture.

After all, it was reasoned, the Chinese expressed over and over again that they wanted to learn Western management practice. However, what Foster's did not anticipate was the flow-on effect of ending banquets. An expatriate manager recalled:

> In winter we used to buy steam, we didn't generate our own steam at the brewery. If there was a steam supply shortage, the brewery would be the first to lose steam. If there was a problem with water, a problem with power, and any issues like that, bang, the brewery was the first one that came off the list and shut down.

Initially, no one realised these problems had anything to do with eating and drinking. The Chinese staff mentioned this at the beginning but the Australians took no notice. The Chinese gave up trying to teach Australians about doing business the Chinese way and decided they would have to learn the hard way. After all, the Australians said they were there to change the culture.

In addition to supply problems, Foster's Shanghai found itself being fined by all sorts of local government bodies for all kinds of reasons, such as poor hygiene conditions outside the front gate of the brewery. It took the expatriate managers 12 months to decide that something, perhaps, needed to be done. The expatriate recalled:

> So after 12 months we did a review of our policy and said, 'this is not working, we need to do a bit of hospitality work', and got back into it. It didn't cost us much in dollars but it meant a huge amount to our suppliers and we were back in the sweet books again. There was some learning there about how the Chinese system works.

Supplying a little gratitude

A suppliers' conference is a typical way of thanking them for their support. In a centrally planned economy where raw material was allocated with a tight ration control, additional supply of raw material meant suppliers reaching or exceeding their levels of approved production. Suppliers' conferences were usually held at a holiday resort once a year. All suppliers were invited and sometimes also potential suppliers. Relationships were secured for the following year. Company representatives were generously wined, dined and entertained. In return, suppliers ensured smooth supply to demonstrate their gratitude.

Foster's Shanghai stopped these suppliers' conferences at the start of the joint venture operation. Constant supply problems forced it to review the policy and conferences were resumed a few years later. By tradition, as with Foster's competitors, conferences were held in a different holiday location each year, all expenses paid. Foster's took advantage of being a joint venture and organised a conference in Hong Kong one year, something their Chinese competitors were not able to do without foreign connections in the early 1990s. This put Foster's ahead of its competitors in securing a smooth supply chain.

Expatriates with only superficial exposure to Chinese culture often suggested banquets were unethical and simply a form of bribery. But in Chinese business culture it is merely an opportunity to establish understanding between parties and build relationships, a way of socialising and building networks.

Banquets do not necessarily have to be extravagant. It is the thought and action that counts. For Australian expatriates, this was a learning process. Some of them, after a few years in China, learnt that banquets are effective tools in business. One expatriate manager who worked in the Guangdong joint venture for a three-year term enjoyed his assignment so much he applied for a second term. He specifically commented on how much he learnt from his first term and how he used food as a business tool successfully.

In his second term he was with the Tianjin joint venture and recalled one specific incident in Tianjin when he resolved supply issues. From his previous time in Guangdong, he established a network with suppliers in Shanghai. While in Tianjin, he tried to help Foster's in Guangdong to get bottles delivered there from a supplier in Shanghai. The supply was not a problem but transportation was. 'We couldn't get any railway wagons to put them into, no matter what the purchasing guy did.'

It was suggested off the cuff that the railway chief wanted to meet the expatriate manager. Having been in China for a few years and understanding the way business worked, he promptly held a banquet for the railway manager. The following day he was told the railway chief liked him, and 'Oh, by the way, there are some wagons free now.' For an Australian expatriate manager, this was magical. It was not the way he would do business in Australia, but in China he had learnt how effective a banquet could be.

There is no shortage of examples of how food is used as an effective tool in doing business in China. The main goal of eating together is to build relationships for the future. On another occasion a supplier of labels for Foster's in the south rescued the same manager by producing labels in Guangzhou and sending them to Tianjin for a cheaper price than from a local producer in Tianjin. This was the result of a relationship cultivated in Doumen, Guangdong, several years earlier on the manager's first assignment.

The 3Rs: Relax, repair and reciprocate

Eating together provides opportunities for parties to repair relationships when they are not going well, or make more progress when they are. Banquets enable discussions on matters that normally would be considered outside the parameters of a business meeting.

Even more importantly, banquets are reciprocated, and foreigners who visit for a short time often misjudge the level of reciprocation and therefore get false impressions about banquets being unethical bribes. This is a typical 'Glass Wall Effect' that often can hold more dangers than having no knowledge at all.

The other common mistake that Western visitors make is to simply accept these invitations as a normal form of hospitality, because they are unfamiliar with the Chinese manner of trying to pay bills in restaurants. Chinese must try absolutely and most sincerely to pay bills at the end by rushing to get money through to the cashier. Chinese will do this so genuinely that they push their friends to the side. Most Western business people offer once or twice and stop when they are politely refused. Western business people should learn how to rush in front of their Chinese colleagues. Trying to pay bills is especially worth practising once you become friendly and familiar with the people you share food with.

Food and culture affect all levels of business operations. As mentioned, the harmonious principles of food are fundamental to Chinese eating and drinking habits, especially linked with seasons and temperature. The Chinese believe that beer has a natural quality of 'coolness' that is good for reducing internal body heat in summer. In Shanghai, especially during the 'huangmei' season, beer is generally consumed by men and women of all ages.

There is a sub-cultural difference that in Beijing it was taboo for women to drink beer at all times, although this has changed greatly in the past 30 years because of the influence of Western culture. On the other hand, in winter, beer consumption is regarded as being harmful to health. Foster's, coming from the Australian culture, where there is little fluctuation in beer consumption between seasons, was not prepared for seasonal fluctuations in production and consumption in China.

It was estimated by one manager that in Shanghai the difference between summer peak months and winter months was as much as a factor of ten. This was a total shock to Foster's, as it was to other international brewers. In Foster's first winter season, it had no idea of the problem and was ill-prepared, with a high level of stock that only had a six-month shelf life.

Using food to the best advantage

Dining at a Chinese banquet requires knowledge and preparation and there are also regional cultural differences. For instance, soup is served at the end of a meal in Beijing, but in Guangzhou it is served at the beginning. Knowledge of how many courses may be served at a banquet is useful so that by the time farinaceous, such as rice or noodles, is served, guests will still be able to have a small amount to complete the meal to ensure the harmony (Lafayette De Mente 1994). Inability to do so shows a poor level of sophistication.

Chinese are also known for the variety of food they eat (Wang 1981), in southern China more so than in the north. Sometimes certain delicacies are not easily accepted by Western business people as they have not previously experienced such food. The correct and polite way of handling food such as snakes, frogs, scorpions and other dishes that are not common dietary items to Westerners is to show enthusiastic appreciation because your host went to great trouble organising it.

In most cases, delicacies are rare and expensive. Your host may have used their network to obtain them. Restaurants that serve these dishes will only tell certain clients rather than having them on the menu. It is not polite to leave a large portion of an expensive dish untouched. It does not show appreciation and your Chinese host will not make the effort for you in the future. To show appreciation, you must at least try. If you really can't handle it, pick it up with your chopsticks, make sure your host notices you are trying, and leave the remaining part on your plate.

There is little literature to teach Westerners the sophisticated eating style of China. But there are hundreds of Chinese publications and courses offered in China to train Chinese how to deal with unsophisticated Westerners. Most organisations have a foreign affairs office or department solely to deal with foreigners. Chinese are often shocked to hear there is no equivalent in Western organisations. I once overheard banquet instructions being given in China by a foreign affairs officer in a car with a delegation that had arrived from Melbourne: 'No intestines or organs', he said, 'we have foreigners.'

Understanding the drinking 'game'

The ability to handle drinking is important in doing business with Chinese. Some Western business people proudly tell me they do not get into the Chinese drinking 'games'. Chinese are very hospitable and polite people and do not force people to drink, especially guests and strangers: to make a guest or stranger drink and get drunk may lead to them losing face by embarrassing themselves.

'Rangjiu (让酒)' (the way to persuade guests to drink more) is different. It is a form of politeness and manners. It is the duty of hosts to ensure guests are properly wined and dined. A direct translation of 'rang' is 'please' and a good host must continue to say 'please (drink or eat more)' throughout the banquet. This communication style of repeating phrases is good manners rather than transmitting a message repeatedly, which may be perceived by Westerners as trying to get them to drink too much.

Drinking can also be a game in business dining. The person who cannot handle the amount of drink and embarrasses themselves first is clearly seen as the weaker party. At different stages of a relationship's development, for example a stage of negotiations, drinking can be used as a game to demonstrate strength. It is not unheard of from Western business people that 'drinkers' were brought in halfway through a banquet. Without knowing the sophistication of Chinese culture, Westerners may misunderstand the intention.

It is the host's duty to ensure guests enjoy themselves to the full extent and part of the culture is not to have a guest drink alone. Therefore, if the guest is a good drinker and the host is not, bringing in others who can drink with guests is good behaviour by the host. This practice enables guests to enjoy as many drinks as they like and no one loses face by not drinking or leaving the guest to drink alone.

However, another way of playing this drinking game is indeed bringing in 'drinkers' to compete. It then becomes a game of showing force and strength. In the process of negotiating joint ventures, Foster's executives experienced this situation. At a number of banquets, 'drinkers' were brought in. To the surprise of their Chinese counterparts, these Australian executives were brewers who had much drinking experience over the years of their career. The games stopped after the Chinese realised the Australians were heavier drinkers.

Western business people sometimes find it difficult to deal with eating and drinking as a business strategy, especially those not familiar with local table manners. One member of a delegation I accompanied to China said he would not drink, to avoid the drinking games. He also ignored all the table etiquette. He simply sat down and ate by himself. He did not wait for the host to put food on his plate and just took what he wanted. There were no intervals as there were no toasts made; hence there were no conversations. As a result, all the meals turned out to be short, dull and boring. Meals were merely used to satisfy hunger.

All cultures evolve

As with all cultures over time, the eating and drinking culture evolves. Today, Chinese festivals are often used as an opportunity to build business relationships. For example, Moon Festival is a very good opportunity to visit customers and clients with boxes of moon cakes. This does not make your action of visiting seem patronising. In some ways it also legitimises the giving of gifts.

Knowledge of Chinese festivals, the meaning of gifts and the right types of gifts can go a long way in successfully doing business with Chinese. Once I was on a mission setting up collaboration with a Chinese institute. The day the Chinese party chose to sign the agreement was Moon Festival. I briefed my senior colleague about it and all the meaningful things such as moon cakes. They represent union and getting together.

My colleague was able to give a speech that began with the significance of signing the agreement on a day when family and friends unite. This signified smooth, successful and long-term corporation and was very well received by the Chinese.

In conclusion, through understanding that the fundamentals of Chinese culture underpin the philosophy and the principle of food, and eating and drinking etiquette, Western business people will find their time dining with Chinese become more enjoyable and successful when food is used as a business tool properly.

References

Anderson, E. N., Jr., 1997, 'Traditional medical values of food in food and culture', in Counihan, C. and Van Esterik, P., eds, *Knowledge and Innovation in the New Service Economy*, pp. 80–93 (New York: Routledge).

Chance, P., 1992, Interpretive restraint and ritual tradition: Marysville's Festival of Bok Kai, *Journal of Contemporary Ethnography* 21, 226–254.

Civitello, L., 2007, *Cuisine and Culture: A History of Food and People* (Hoboken, NJ: John Wiley).

Chung, M., 2008, *Shanghaied: Why Foster's Could Not Survive China* (Heidelberg Press, Melbourne).

Cooper, E., 1986, The Chinese table manners: you are how you eat, *Human Organization* 45(2), 179–184.

Gray, J. H., 2003, *China: A History of the Laws, Manners and Customs of the People* (Mineola, NY: Dover Publications).

Hofstede, G., 2001, *Culture's Consequences*, 2nd edn (Thousand Oaks: Sage Publications).

Lafayette De Mente, B., 1994, *Chinese Etiquette and Ethics in Business* (Chicago, IL: NTC Business Books).

Lai, T. C., 1978, *Chinese Food for Thought* (Hong Kong: Hong Kong Book Centre).

Ludman, E., and Newman, J., 1984, Yin and yang in the health related food practices of three Chinese groups, *Journal of Nutrition Education* 16, 3–5.

Simmons, F. J., 1991, *Food in China: A Cultural and Historical Inquiry* (New York: CRC Press).

Swanson, L. A., 1996, Billion mouths to feed: Food linguistics and cross-cultural, cross-"national" food consumption habits in China, *British Food Journal* 98(6), 33.

Tan, S. P., and Wheeler, E., 1988, Concepts relating to health and food held by Chinese women in London, *Ecology of Food and Nutrition* 13, 43.

Visser, M., 1991, *The Rituals of Dinner – the Origins, Evolution, Eccentricties, and Meaning of Table Manners* (Toronto: Penguin Books).

Wan, J. Z. 万., 1994, 饮食与中国文化: 江西高校出版社.

Wang, A., 1981, Chinese traditional food therapy, *Journal of the American Dietetic Association*, 10, 55–57.

Wang, R. X. 王, 1993, 饮食与中国文化. 北京: 人民出版社.

Yau, O., 1994, *Consumer Behaviour in China: Customer Satisfaction and Cultural Values* (New York: Routledge).

10

How to market products to Chinese consumers

Abstract: This chapter discusses one of the most critical and sensitive topics today in selling goods to Chinese – cross-cultural marketing. It seems an irony that the fundamental of marketing taught in any marketing course is satisfying the customers' needs and wants. However, when it comes to marketing to Chinese, MNCs seem to have a different idea about what products the Chinese consumers should consume which is usually according to the MNCs.

Without the understanding of the Chinese market and consumers, Foster's could hardly make a go in the Chinese market.

This chapter discusses many of the unique market characteristics of Chinese market as well as Chinese consumers. By highlighting these differences, future operations may be able to learn some Chinese ways of marketing in China.

Key words: cross-cultural marketing, Western marketing theory, Chinese market, Chinese consumers, potential of China, market entry, feasibility study and market research, cultural knowledge of the Chinese market, brands, brand names in Chinese, packaging and labelling, distribution, local marketing knowledge, promotion communication for Chinese, Shanghai Dragon Girl, personal selling, cultural behaviour.

Multinational companies around the world went into the Chinese market for a simple reason: its 1.3 billion consumers.

From purely a strategy viewpoint this has proven to be unsuccessful, simply because of the cultural complexity of China's vast mass of potential customers. Without culturally suited marketing strategies, billions of dollars were poured into China and it became a giant black hole for many marketers. This chapter looks at why it is essential when marketing products to the Chinese to take cultural differences into consideration. It draws on research by the author into the Foster's Group experience of three joint ventures with Chinese breweries from 1993 to 2006.

Culturally suited strategies are essential

All marketing activities, anywhere, begin with an analysis of the market and a process of formulating strategies and plans, according to all trained marketers and their text books. Some argue that setting up the right strategies is crucial to success in international business; others believe the implementation of strategy is more important. It is argued here that establishing correct strategies is a prerequisite for adequate implementation.

The first stage of the Foster's marketing strategy was relatively simple: give the Chinese partners the sales and marketing functions. This soon proved to be ineffective and various other strategies were implemented. Foster's believed that its Chinese partners had all the knowledge of the market and it only had to ensure a quality product; that in a market where product quality was often inconsistent, producing consistent quality would be a strong competitive advantage.

This was the first initiative and the task was given to a large team of expatriate Australians looking after operations in Shanghai and Guangdong, using quality ingredients. However, the strategy dramatically increased product unit costs and was soon found not to be feasible. Sales did not grow as expected and strategies were reviewed. The Chinese sales representatives had wide knowledge of the local market and consumers, but this was limited to local products. Foster's was an international brand and it was necessary to sell it at a premium price. To create, expand and sustain an international premium brand image, the product had to be sold at a premium consistent with international rivals. This strategy was sound in theory, but in a market where disposable income was limited it was inevitable that sales were small and it was difficult to grow the market.

To apply modern Western marketing theories to the market, young Australian graduates with good language skills were employed to head the marketing of these premium brands. But they lacked the commercial experience and, especially, knowledge of Chinese business culture and Chinese consumers. These were crucial in dealing with local employees, suppliers and customers. At the same time, in a culture where age is respected, the local Chinese staff were uncomfortable being supervised by young expatriate Australian managers with little knowledge, skills and experience in the Chinese market.

Having trialled the strategy of using expatriates without success, Foster's belatedly recognised the importance of language and culture, and brought in overseas Chinese from Hong Kong, Taiwan, Singapore, Canada and elsewhere, in another attempt to introduce Western sales and marketing concepts and processes. Market research was initially conducted by Hong Kong firms, but many Hong Kong marketing professionals did not like living and working in China. A day-trip was often the only effort they made locally to understand the Chinese market.

After this strategy also failed, marketing support was sought from the Foster's head office in Australia. Pursuing a policy of uniformity of products and marketing activities, the head office marketing department then helped to implement strategies used across all sections at Foster's International. This produced a global image of the Foster's brand but the complexity of the Chinese market meant that securing improved sales was slow in the short term. To many marketers this meant their careers were unlikely to progress by working in China; hence there was a high turnover of young marketing professionals.

The attraction of China

Chinese market entry strategy was implemented at a time when Foster's was experiencing a decline in its Australian market as well as in the UK (the UK brewing business, Courage, was sold in 1995). The China entry was part of a broader Asian strategy that focused on markets with significant growth opportunities, rather than simply continuing to compete in mature markets such as Europe and America.

Foster's research in the early 1990s indicated that per capita consumption of beer in China was expected to grow quickly, and that China would become the world's largest beer market by 2000, and would become a larger market for Foster's than Australia. It was also estimated that China's beer market was the second largest in the world (behind America) in 1993. Meanwhile, in the early 1990s, the Chinese Government recognised that the beer industry was in urgent need of updating, especially in technology and management, and was under-resourced. Attracting foreign direct investment was a major solution.

Background work by Foster's for its China investment began in late 1991 and was ahead of most other international brewers. By 1993, the year before Foster's China was established, a Shanghai Foster's brewery feasibility study noted there were only six deals (mostly joint ventures) in progress. By 1997 there were at least 88 joint venture or licensing agreements signed with Chinese breweries.

The level of competition among domestic brewers was not as intense in the early 1990s as later because there were few international breweries in the market. They brought international standards of brewing to China, which was the Foster's strategy for major product differentiation. This quality approach ensured there would be little competition in the market other than from international players and a few Chinese.

But Foster's was aware this was likely to change rapidly. Indeed, other major international brands went into China either at the same time or just after Foster's. Very quickly, Heineken, Carlsberg, Budweiser, Suntory and others were competing with each other. Even major Chinese brands joined the competition. Qingdao is a good example, a national beer brand that has become an international brand.

Foster's saw the potential market growth and the lack of a unified international standard in China. Having a brand that was already established worldwide, Foster's Lager, it believed it was in a strong position to compete with the majority of Chinese breweries, of which there were more than 800 across the country at the time. The strategy to have a competitive advantage through consistent quality was easily achieved because of strong technical resources. However, in a market where consumers did not know the difference between consistent and inconsistent quality, it made no difference.

It also used the Foster's brand as a major competitive tool, even though as a successful international brand it was less well known in China than, say, Heineken.

Exporting, licensing agreements, joint ventures and subsidiaries were the main methods used by Foster's when entering international markets and building brands. Foster's focused on manufacturing in China for several reasons:

1. The growth potential required a large manufacturing base.

2. High duties would not make importing worthwhile in the long term.

3. Tight government control used a quota system on imported luxury products.

4. A manufacturing base in China could potentially service neighbouring Asian countries.

Reports from consultants in Hong Kong suggested potential market growth was huge and rapid, so importing would not be cost effective.

Licensing agreements were not considered suitable for China for three main reasons. First, China had an unsophisticated legal system to protect commercial parties. Second, the low industry standards suggested there would be a very limited number of breweries capable of fulfilling the role; and those that might produce Foster's brand at the required quality were large national breweries and not interested in licensing arrangements because they were direct competitors. Third, using smaller Chinese breweries would mean substantial training, at great cost, to reach the required quality. This could potentially introduce competitors into the market at a later date.

Joint ventures the only suitable vehicle

Foster's considered joint ventures as the only sound strategy because it believed its Chinese partners had the best local knowledge of the market. It is still common for companies to rush into China without thorough planning. In the early 1990s companies were more concerned about missing opportunities than spending time doing their homework.

In less than a year, between 1992 and 1993, Foster's conducted site analyses at more than a dozen breweries scattered throughout China, but these audits only focused on technical elements. The list of available breweries was also limited. For instance, Guangdong Foster's in Doumen was considered a bad purchase by many executives. In addition, Foster's executives believed that joint ventures were the only form of ventures permitted by the Chinese Government, when in reality they were encouraged, whereas wholly foreign-owned enterprises were permitted but not encouraged.

The lack of preparation has not improved among Australian companies. More recent research found an alarmingly large number of companies did not do proper homework before entering China.

There is no doubt that market research by Foster's was not thorough enough and its planning was inadequate. Accurate information plays an essential role in planning processes (Ehrman and Hamburg 1986). In countries such as China, where there is great cultural diversity, correct collection of data is relatively more difficult than in countries with few internal cultural differences. The planning process will also take longer, relative to the availability of data-collecting facilities, and of primary and secondary data.

In 1992 and 1993, initial market research was often carried out by Austrade or students who lacked a systematic professional approach. Furthermore, without a national infrastructure for market research in China, it was difficult for Foster's to determine the quality of research. My research in 2008 showed that data mining was conducted by Melbourne-based companies mainly through researching on the Internet. The researchers were usually university graduates with no knowledge of China and the Chinese market.

Two major problems are highlighted by this process. First, the data that is published and approved by the Chinese agencies should only be used as a reference, because of the level of its accuracy. Second, graduates without any knowledge of China simply cannot judge the usefulness and relevance of data collected.

It is reasonable to conclude that for Foster's to base major decisions on limited research results, it was likely to lead to inappropriate strategies in building brands. It is also reasonable to suggest that the entry decision by Foster's was rushed and therefore difficult to execute. Indeed, deciding on joint venture entry did cause big operational difficulties later on.

An Australian 'flying squad' approach

To search for suitable locations, Foster's used an initial 'flying squad' of Carlton & United Breweries employees for research and site analyses to find potential joint venture partners. Four main geographical locations were identified as essential: Guangdong, Beijing, Shanghai and Sichuan. Initial feasibility studies showed the three areas with significant growth in beer sales were Beijing, Guangdong and Shandong. Shanghai's sales growth rate was one of the slowest in 1991, at 5.3 per cent compared to an average of 21.86 per cent across the country.

Other studies found that greater Guangdong and greater Shanghai were two prime areas of higher GDP growth (Frewen and Mosely 1995). Therefore, the decision to invest in the Shanghai market was also a sound decision.

In the meantime, technical auditing of a large number of breweries, mainly by the flying squad, gave Foster's opportunities to understand many aspects of China's market. Several leading national brands, such as Qingdao, Yanjing and Five Star, had good brand image and value. Qingdao was and still is the main export brand. It is now listed on the stock exchange and is the largest brewery in China. Yanjing is nominated as the official drink for state banquets.

Apart from these top brands, the industry as a whole lacked quality and consistency. Across the board, breweries used low-quality raw materials to produce beer cheaply. At the time of Foster's entry, few industry standards were imposed on brewers and suppliers' standards were segmented and inconsistent along geographical lines.

A good example of the industry problems is beer bottles, to demonstrate not only standards and inconsistency in supplies but also the regional differences in the beer industry as a whole. China's bottle returns system determines the packaging system. Bottles are returned to the manufacturer via retailers and distributors. Manufacturers rely on this but it is up to consumers to return bottles at their leisure and receive a small refund.

Bottles are specially manufactured to take the pressure of the gas in the beer but there is no system to check that only beer bottles are returned; retailers accept any bottles of a similar shape and size. When other types are returned, soy sauce bottles for example, accidents and injuries have resulted from refilling with beer.

On establishing the Shanghai joint venture, Foster's put a great deal of effort into meeting suppliers of all types of material, because the Australian manager very quickly recognised the importance of relationships to the smooth day-to-day running of the business. With little experience in a totally different culture, the importance of supplier–manufacturer relationships was not widely recognised by Foster's management for about a year.

Lack of knowledge leads to nasty surprises

In an effort to gain a broad knowledge of the market before entry, Foster's used two main sources of information: a market definition study done by internal resources, and a feasibility study purchased from a Hong Kong firm. The latter's level of usefulness was an issue. Figures were mainly on the basis of certain assumptions; for instance, the growth of market size was based on population, with little consideration of other economic and social factors (for example, the level of disposable income in relation to the ability of consumers to buy a premium product).

The feasibility reports appeared to be mass produced to cater for all customers in the same industry. As a result, international brewers who purchased similar reports appear to have adopted similar strategies.

What was fundamentally lacking was consumer information about cultural characteristics. For example, at no time was Foster's prepared for the seasonal fluctuations of the Chinese beer market. This was simply because all of them only had knowledge of the Australian market. Management, marketers and operations managers were all shocked by the different sales figures between seasons. The Chinese believe that beer has a natural quality of coolness that is good for reducing internal body heat in summer, but in winter this damages health. A high level of health consciousness is an important part of Chinese culture, which is deeply reflected in cuisine.

The beer consumption pattern in China was totally foreign to Foster's and all international brewers. It was estimated by one manager that in Shanghai the difference between summer peak months and winter months was as high as a factor of 10.

This distinct consumer culture caused further problems in distribution, warehousing, production, packaging, supply and general management. In both Shanghai and Guangzhou, several warehouses were established to hold stock in the quieter season in the hope of building an adequate supply for the peak season. But this created large storage costs and a stock rotation problem (the use-by date). Foster's and international brewers strictly followed the standard of six months' product shelf life.

In packaging, for example, further capital investment went into purchasing additional bottles to overcome problems with the returns system. But because it was an industry-wide system rather than manufacturer based, additional bottles simply went into the system and benefited other manufacturers.

There was also a culturally related characteristic of consumption by geographical location. Beer drinking is associated with blue-collar culture in the north (Beijing and Tianjin) but class is less of a concern in southern China (Shanghai and Guangdong). This created challenges in market penetration and marketing the brand, especially for marketers who only had experience of one market type, such as Australia or Hong Kong. This lack of experience in marketing in different cultures led to unsuitable and ineffective strategies.

Accurate market research a major challenge

In the early 1990s, the concept of marketing was fairly new to all Chinese consumers, which presented opportunities and challenges. In May 1996 Foster's used a range of research specialists, including Guangdong White Horse Marketing Research (a joint venture), Shanghai Modern International Research (which produced hand-written briefs in English), the George Patterson agency, and marketing personnel from Carlton & United Breweries.

Guangdong White Horse, a Chinese firm that conducted a major research project for Foster's, was capable of presenting briefs and reports in English of a standard close to what would be expected from any firm in Australia. Shanghai Modern International Research appeared to be behind in its standard and presentation but had a basic understanding of general market research methods commonly used by other firms. George Patterson produced standard market research documentation as expected. The final report, however, was produced by the Carlton & United Breweries marketing team in head office, using raw data from the other research.

The research was of a qualitative nature, carried out by local Chinese research staff in Shanghai, where the respondents were sourced. Lack of appropriate skills by local researchers was recognised as a concern by the Foster's research team, but the need to conduct research in the local dialect was important to gather data. It is questionable whether the research was conducted to the requirement of Foster's and that the data collected was as useful as it could have been.

Processes were observed by Foster's marketing people and the research reports were not used directly to influence decision-making. The reports produced by the head office team incorporated some of the most useful research data. A manager commented: 'Unfortunately the Chinese researchers in those earlier days were not into non-directed consumer focus groups. They would actually probably watch the process go through, not understanding the need for non-directive input.'

The Chinese researchers would direct the respondents during the focus groups. This is generally considered as leading. Compared to purchasing costly research reports from Hong Kong firms, this research at least presented the benefits of selecting real informant samples from the consumer-base population. Nevertheless, unfortunately very little understanding of the market was obtained before full Foster's operations started in China.

Evaluating information was difficult, in the early days especially, when relatively poor-quality data was presented and expatriates had little contextual knowledge to evaluate it. When research was carried out by students, Foster's made an effort to confirm the data but that was 'not very effective,' one marketer recalls. In later years, Foster's had no choice but to use Chinese market research firms, with unsatisfactory results.

These limitations were beyond the control of Foster's in terms of supply and quality of the data and this created difficulties in information evaluation and decision-making.

The brands conundrum

Foster's has a range of very successful brands in Australia. The brand that dominates the Victorian market is Victoria Bitter, known as VB. Internationally, Foster's Group consciously promotes Foster's Lager, a successful strategy in other overseas markets, such as America and Europe. In 2005 Foster's (led by Foster's Lager) was the seventh-largest international premium brand by volume, the second-largest brand in the UK, and among the top ten in Western Europe.

The price factor forced Foster's to operate differently in China because Foster's could only be a premium brand to achieve profitability. The initial strategy was to purchase local brands from breweries, form joint ventures, stop producing the local brands and then produce only Foster's Lager. The strategy proved to be inadequate because the size of the premium beer market was not as large as Foster's had hoped and there was fierce international competition.

Foster's recognised that a range of brands was needed and three levels were developed: international premium brand (Foster's Lager and Foster's Ice); a Chinese premium brand (Shanghai Dragon, which was exported from Shanghai to Europe and Australia); and local brands.

In Shanghai, the Chinese partner had two brands that covered different market segments. Guangming was, and still is, a commodity product with a strong consumer following. It was the mainstay for Huaguang brewery for many years and it soon came to serve a similar role in the joint venture. Huaguang's premium brand was Shanghai beer (relaunched later as Shanghai Dragon) and Shanghai Foster's Brewery continued to build it into a sub-premium brand, but it has never taken off.

Foster's also decided that an international launch was needed for Shanghai Dragon to sell it in Europe, so a new marketing campaign was developed, again by George Patterson, the Australian market research and advertising firm.

The Shanghai Dragon Girl promotion was launched in 1998. By 2004, Shanghai Beer as a brand was taken out of the local commodity range and put in the premium portfolio. However, the Shanghai Dragon Girl advertisement was rejected by the Chinese marketers, although it was briefly used in London and Taiwan. It produced no real noticeable results. The promotion is analysed further in this chapter.

The Foster's head office marketing team acknowledged after ten years of struggling in the Shanghai market that Foster's was too strong for Chinese consumers and that this had been the major difficulty in selling it. A Foster's executive commented:

> Foster's is less relevant to them than brands that were seen to be even more modern, or have more heritage from Europe, or high quality or overtly high quality in an image status context. So what held us back all those years was that we as marketers were not prepared to take those things on board and tailor-make Foster's Lager for China. But it did result finally in us deciding to launch a line extension to Foster's Lager, called Foster's Ice.

Foreign brands were unfamiliar to the Chinese consumers; therefore marketing education was necessary but this required time. Many European brands, Heineken for example, are seen by Chinese consumers as high quality even though they are produced in China, often to a different local specification. On the other hand, Foster's was not known to Chinese consumers. Australia was not a country as large (economically) as the US or as well known as European countries such as the UK or Germany. Therefore to educate Chinese consumers about an Australian brand, Foster's first had to educate them about Australia.

In Doumen, the Chinese partner was already producing Huangmei (Princess) and Huangmei Fruit Beer (a specialty product for the Hainan market made of half beer and half fruit juice). Both had a strong presence in Hainan Island, with about 30 per cent of the market there.

Foster's Lager was launched in June 1995, two years after the establishment of the joint ventures and at a time when many other international brands were being launched. Foster's wanted a head start. Foster's Lager did not yield the expected results, so two additional brands, Power's and Eazy, were created and launched in the Guangdong market. They were launched early in 1997 in readiness for the peak summer season.

Eazy was created for the lucrative Guangzhou market, which was the initial target for Guangzhou Foster's Brewery. Visually, its design resembled a Hong Kong-style beer, which was seen as desirable by Guangdong consumers, and was a lighter beer with a preferred less-bitter taste. Power's was a relaunch of an old Queensland favourite and chosen for the Hainan market as an Australian-style beer.

In Tianjin, the joint venture had its original brand, Great Wall, which was discontinued as soon as the old Tianjin brewery was closed. In its place, two new brands were created, Largo and Witz. Largo became an instant success in a market where there was no competition and within two to three months was the market leader. Its price was pitched at about 1.3 yuan a bottle, a very low price that locals could afford. It was recognised that a local brand at a commodity price was necessary.

After Foster's had been in China for ten years, the general situation in the brewing industry had changed. By 2004, the total number of breweries in China had fallen from more than 800 to 200 and the nature of competition had changed. Importantly, surviving breweries have also changed industry standards for the better. Now international standards are fundamental and consistency of quality is expected, even for local brands.

Previously, only a handful of international players had been competitors. Today, all surviving breweries compete, whether they are international or Chinese. This increased competition has created areas of difficulty for companies, for instance in branding, pricing and distribution networks.

Multi-level strong international brands require strong financial backing in promotion, because price competition restricts profit margins and there are still limitations on distribution networks for certain geographical locations.

Disastrous brand names by characters

An area of distinct cultural difference between the West and China is the degree of care given to choosing a brand name. In the West, a name is a symbol, a sign that is used to distinguish one product from another. In China, a name is more than just a symbol and a sign. It must have a meaning.

In the Chinese language, words with the same sound or tone may be represented by totally different characters, which carry totally different meanings. For a brand name, not only must the characters be chosen to represent a meaning, but also the sound of the characters must be carefully considered. An added difficulty is the different pronunciation used in different dialects for the same word.

When Foster's beer was first sold in Hong Kong, the brand name was translated into Huoshida 霍士达. It is meant to have a close sound to the English word Foster's by pronunciation. In Cantonese this set of sounds does not have any significant meaning.

The first character Huo (霍) is merely a surname and shida (士达) were just characters with the closest sound to the English in Cantonese. They have no real meaning. When pronounced in Mandarin, Huoshida (霍士达) shares the same sound as (祸事达), which means 'the disasters just arrived'. It is not difficult to understand why consumers would not buy the product. The name was changed later to Fushida (富士达), which was not intended to carry any meaning. However the choice of Chinese characters was wrong: 富士 was also used in Fuji Mountain (富士山). Chinese consumers know about Japan and the Japanese, and immediately associated Fushida (富士达) with Fuji Mountain and took Foster's to be a Japanese brand. There is a strong cultural resentment among Chinese towards the Japanese because of the Chinese–Japanese war (1937–1945).

Suntory, a Japanese company, named its beer xili (喜力). That does not resemble the sound of Suntory but the characters bear the meaning of 'happy energy', which is acceptable to consumers and gives no indication of its Japanese origin. Budweiser chose Baiwei (百威), which means 'a hundred times impressive strength' and faintly resembles the sound of Budweiser.

China is more like Europe than America when it comes to languages. In America, people speak English with distinct accents but have little difficulty understanding each other. In China, there are 292 officially listed languages and many dialects are so different that people refer to them as different languages. For instance, Cantonese and Shanghainese are very different from Mandarin, so much so that people speaking the different dialects cannot understand each other.

Although Foster's was the fourth-largest brewery (Shanghai Foster's Brewery, 1993) at the time of the joint venture's formation, in 2003 it was number 22 in the world and Foster's was not a well-known brand in China. Indeed, after being in the Chinese market for more than ten years, it was still unclear how well Foster's was known as a brand or an Australian brand. This clearly showed the failure of its marketing exercise.

Being part of a large and culturally diverse country, Chinese consumers assign great significance to products from specific geographical locations. Yet little consideration was given by Foster's to the exact geographical location of the breweries. Guangzhou Foster's Brewery soon discovered that a brand from Doumen, a small county, would not sell in large cities such as Guangzhou, because city people would not drink 'peasants' products'. Guangzhou Foster's chose to register itself in Zhuhai, to be able to sell its products in Guangzhou.

Packaging and labelling the Chinese way

Like other multinational companies, Foster's has its own guidelines on packaging and labelling as part of its branding exercise. These are a means of ensuring consistency of brand image and value, and product quality. The ability and quality of packaging material suppliers are key elements for consistent packaging and labelling of any product. From the beginning, Foster's recognised the importance of packaging and expatriate packaging managers were appointed to all three China plants.

The beer industry in China had low-quality packaging standards. For Foster's, the practice of recycling bottles through production was not only below industry standards in terms of image, but also against health and safety regulations in countries such as Australia. To address such issues and establish the Foster's brand, the joint ventures invested heavily in packaging and labelling.

In analysis of the cause of the relatively unsuccessful sales compared with other international brands, it was suggested by some that Chinese consumers were not keen on the colour blue. This line of thought was not shared by the marketing team in Melbourne, because Pepsi is a successful brand in China and its dominant label colour is dark blue, similar to Foster's Lager. However, Asian consumers found the design of the label was somewhat confusing. A former Melbourne manager commented:

> When I used to travel through Singapore, in the first-class business lounge I was forever taking Foster's out of the softdrink fridge. The Foster's label design does not have an appearance of a traditional beer to many Asians, but resembles a softdrink. It is a combination of many factors, the logo, the colour and everything else that doesn't have a beer look.

The need to adapt packaging and labelling is not an alien concept to companies marketing international brands. 'Foster's Lager', the text on the label, created difficulty in the Asian market as it does not say beer, so the word beer was added. The great success of Foster's in Australia and other countries led to arrogance about the brand and product, according to some Foster's people interviewed. A Chinese manager said: 'It is such a good brand with good quality. It was not a slightest thought to Foster's that people would not buy it; Chinese must all want to drink Foster's.'

A major difficulty for Foster's in selling its product was the taste. Foster's was proud of its product, which has a strong hopsy taste. But this was not a taste that Chinese consumers were used to. Many other international brands gradually introduced light beer and found that more suited to Chinese consumers' taste. Foster's resisted until 2003 and launched Foster's Ice, a beer with a lighter taste and colour, and a label of a different colour. However, the success of Bud Ice gave Budweiser a substantial market share in Shanghai. However, Foster's Ice, although a similar product in the same market, was not a success.

Distribution swings, roundabouts and roadblocks

Distribution is much less straightforward in China compared to developed countries and was possibly the most difficult area for Foster's because of market characteristics and lack of a distribution infrastructure. A major surprise for all executives was probably the alien nature of China's distribution systems, which were a product of a centrally planned economy. The well-established Foster's distribution structure in Australia had been built for a market economy. A Melbourne executive explained: 'Carlton & United Breweries built its own distribution. This is why the business was so good. It owned all the pubs and therefore it created its own distribution . . . that's how Victoria was built up and even Australia.'

Distribution was not a problem faced by Foster's alone, but one that was recognised by other international firms. It has been suggested that distribution is the biggest operational problem that international companies have to deal with in China (Frewen and Mosely 1995).

197

China was a totally different proposition for all Western executives. There was an inefficient distribution system and it was not easy to build your own. Regulations supported a centrally controlled economy, and distribution systems were carefully planned and built up by the Government. Foster's knowledge of building and running a distribution system was almost useless in such an environment. Another factor is the specific nature of the Chinese market, in which distribution is confined to geographical locations. Overcoming this is difficult, perhaps for political reasons, so the selection of an initial geographical base will influence the effectiveness of distribution.

At the start of the China project, a Melbourne beverages export manager was partially involved in the flying squad in the hope of setting up marketing and distribution channels. He visited China many times and commented: 'In hindsight, I should not have been sent. What did I know about China? It is so different to anything we know. I was given an interpreter. The interpreter said yes and no and I was told yes and no. I didn't really know whether it was yes or no.'

He was responsible for setting up the Hong Kong sales office, where he recruited a Hong Kong Chinese who had strong beliefs about recruiting Chinese staff to compensate for Australians' ignorance of Chinese culture. Until 2003, the Hong Kong office was a major sales and marketing base for Foster's China, and marketing strategies for China were designed there by experts from Hong Kong and Australia.

In Hong Kong, sales were customarily achieved by paying a 'tap fee' at a retail outlet, determined according to sales volume. These outlets were generally large customers who did not engage distributors. Marketing was according to Foster's guidelines, providing many standard lines, display fridges, point-of-sales promotion, glasses and other accessories.

In the early years of the joint ventures, Foster's had little choice but to use the strictly regulated distribution channels set up by the Ministry of Light Industry. Manufacturers could not act as wholesalers or distributors. Australian expertise in distribution had very little value and it was a wise decision to leave distribution to the Chinese partners. What Foster's did not understand was the need to match the distribution channels to the products. Huaguang brewery's commodity brand was Guangming, a product for the Shanghai market. It was mainly sold in the western suburbs, where the population was mainly workers with low disposable income. The retail price was 1.5 yuan (about 25 Australian cents) a bottle.

Foster's was an international brand with a different cost base, reflected in its retail price of about 5 yuan a bottle, in line with other international brands. The Foster's and Guangming brands were targeted at different market segments, so the existing distribution channels were not entirely suitable for both. When the joint ventures were formed, none had suitable distribution channels for their premium brands. Initially, distribution expertise was sought within the joint ventures, but it was soon apparent that the existing system was ineffective.

When transport infrastructure means bicycles

In Guangdong, distribution was quickly given to several large distributors based in Zhuhai (a newly developed economic zone in Guangdong near the border with Hong Kong), whereas previously a range of smaller Huangmei distributors had been used. But retailers, often small, had to pick up stock from Zhuhai and this created additional costs and inconvenience.

So although Huangmei was the best-selling brand for many existing retailers, it was too difficult to obtain once stock was concentrated in the hands of several larger distributors, especially when transport infrastructure often came down to using bicycles. Haizhu, the main competitor at the time, grabbed the opportunity and delivered to any retailers who could not pick up the Foster's Princess or Huangmei brands stock from Zhuhai.

The inability to sell enough products of any brands in Guangdong had seen the total production of the Doumen plant fall to 20,000 tonnes in 1998, compared with 40,000 to 50,000 tonnes before the joint venture. Sales promotions and new brand launches became the only hope of reviving Doumen. Through arrogance, naivety or insufficient market research, Australia's largest brewing company had paid a high price for adopting a marketing strategy where it was assumed that if a good product was made, people would rush to buy it.

Following later changes from a centrally planned economy to a market-driven one, the distribution system in China was liberalised. Some distribution channels were allowed to become privately owned to improve efficiency and organisations were permitted to select more suitable and cost-efficient distributors. By 2003, Foster's could select distributors based on their infrastructure, financial capability, the other brands they carried, transportation and relationships with local government.

In 2004, a Shanghai sales office was established to take advantage of further changes expected from China joining the World Trade Organization. No real result came from this exercise either.

The power of local marketing knowledge

It has been highlighted previously that local market knowledge is the most important element in marketing and is fundamental to any organisation's success, but it is a very complex concept, especially when applied across cultures. Unlike most knowledge management literature, De Long and Fahey (2000) have defined knowledge into three types: human knowledge, social knowledge and structured knowledge, as distinct from the more commonly recognised categories of tacit and explicit knowledge. De Long and Fahey facilitate a better understanding of the process of knowledge transfer.

Knowledge in general is created in a certain social setting and regulated by a certain structure, that is, an organisational structure. De Long and Fahey assert that in the process of marketing, knowledge transfer, human knowledge and social knowledge overwhelm structured knowledge.

In Shanghai, the Foster's strategy was to develop its own marketing channels through professional young sales people; for Guangdong brewery, one major distributor was appointed in Zhuhai and Hainan; in Tianjin, products were mainly distributed through Tianjin Foster's Brewery.

The retail structure in China was so different from Australia: large numbers of small outlets that sold small volume. As one expatriate put it: 'Carlton & United Breweries was used to selling truck loads, not bicycle loads.' Small retailers were so financially weak that offers of fees, signs and promotional activities were all extremely attractive to them. At a time when many international brewers were pouring into the Chinese market, there was no shortage of promotional dollars and small retailers quickly learnt how to have their neon signs made free. A Foster's manager recalls:

> They were giving too much away. Others were putting in $10,000 neon signs at the front of what I call little milk bars selling one case of beer. They kept saying, Where's my neon sign? Because they were spoilt they got a neon sign. Basically they just used you as lights, to light up the street.

In short, Foster's did not leverage well on their existing brand value when transferring it into China. This was because China's different cultural system prevented certain values from being transferred.

Local market on a global scale

China is such a large country of segmented markets that the cultural differences between these segments are as great as they are between Australia and China. Not surprisingly, this added further distribution problems for the joint ventures. Knowledge gained from one brewery, for example Guangdong, had little value for operations at the others. It was mostly a case of local problem, local solution.

For example, at Hainan Island, the Princess brand distribution was dominated by a company owned by three brothers. One had a monopoly on distribution of beer, another controlled the return of bottles. Having a large percentage of the product sold in Hainan without the bottles being returned could place Guangzhou Foster's Brewery in serious financial jeopardy.

Within the permission of government policies, both direct and indirect distribution channels were used, depending on which was more suitable and effective. In Guangzhou, a sales office and several warehouses were established to distribute the products. In Shanghai, three warehouses were established between 1996 and 1998 to maintain inventory levels. In Tianjin, at its peak, trucks lined up outside the brewery when it was operating at full capacity.

When intensive distribution was more effective, as in Tianjin, it was adopted as best practice. In Guangdong, selective distribution was implemented and that strategy was sound. In Tianjin there was no competitor, so intensive distribution provided coverage of the market. In Guangzhou there were many other international brands, so Foster's needed to select areas such as Guangzhou and Zhuhai to market its premium brand.

Intensive distribution is relatively expensive, especially in China because the culture emphasises building relationships among employees, suppliers and customers. Entertaining costs money but is effective and necessary.

Effective promotional communication

Promotional communication can only be effective if its objectives are clearly defined. Promotion for sales or marketing is different but it is not uncommon for sales and marketing objectives not to be clearly identified, because focus at first is on distribution to consumers; then the needs and wants of consumers can be addressed, based on market research. A Foster's manager explained: 'Marketing and sales kind of got muddied. Did we want marketing or did we want sales? We really wanted sales because we had some good brands, like Shanghai, which is an excellent brand.'

In marketing concepts, sales and marketing are clearly distinguished as the fundamentals of marketing. According to Kotler and co-workers (1998), marketing is the managing of markets to bring about exchanges for the purpose of satisfying human needs and wants. Sales, however, is about moving the products from the manufacturers to the customers.

In 1992, marketing was still a relatively new concept in China. It was really distribution, how to get the products to the customers. The initial decision to leave sales and marketing to the Chinese partners did bring satisfactory results.

In 2010, organisations often enjoy their marketing efforts implemented when they first entered the Chinese market. For example, Dove is the largest chocolate brand in China. This is because Dove did a lot of advertising, especially in its early days there. Through promotional communication it managed to establish a strong brand image in Chinese consumers' minds. This is referred to by Chinese today as the 'eye-ball' economy, meaning once they see it they will buy it.

The uniqueness of Chinese culture presented operational practices that were difficult for the Australians to comprehend. For example, at the Doumen plant, purchasing was performed by sales personnel provided by the Chinese partner. At one management meeting they were discussing a fall in production caused by wet coal. The Australian general manager was totally confused because he could not see how the two topics could be linked. The decrease in production was caused by purchasing wet coal, which was cheaper but did not burn as well, less steam was generated and therefore production volume was reduced.

For the Chinese, the principle behind purchasing, being a part of the sales team's duty, was to ensure they spent only what was earned through sales. Buying lower-quality raw material was standard practice in China's brewing and other industries as a result of the centrally planned economy

(Purves 1991). It was a way of controlling costs yet still producing the same quantity of product. A direct consequence was that products were not of consistent quality.

Unfortunately for Foster's, sales did not increase with the improvement in product quality. In response, a special marketing research project was carried out between 1994 and 1996 under the control of the marketing department at head office in Melbourne. Chinese market research companies were engaged, and a report on new marketing strategies was presented.

These efforts did not come to fruition because of radical changes at board level on the direction of investment strategy, a general lack of confidence in the Chinese market, and pressure from shareholders. A sales and marketing manager was appointed at the time and a personal-selling strategy was implemented on a small scale in Shanghai, with good results.

The Hong Kong way is not Chinese

This was replaced by the next approach, which involved using Hong Kong marketing and sales firms, in the belief that if Australians could not gain market share and the mainland Chinese did not have enough training and knowledge, then Hong Kong Chinese must be able to succeed.

Thus Foster's attempted to apply Hong Kong sales and marketing knowledge to mainland China. The delusion was that Chinese who spoke Mandarin were Chinese, and if they were Chinese and spoke Chinese, they would also understand the Chinese market.

Stanley Cheung was born in Taiwan, raised in America and was a Foster's executive in China when interviewed. He did not believe that Hong Kong marketing experts were suitable because they lacked a fundamental understanding of the nature of the Chinese market: 'He is from Hong Kong, lives in Hong Kong, works in Hong Kong and goes to China once in a while. I actually lived and worked in Tianjin for about a year.'

Cheung's view was shared by other executives at Shanghai Foster's: 'These (in Hong Kong) didn't want to come to China anyway. If they could, they would fly in in the morning and out at night, rather than spend one more day in China. This is typical of the Hong Kong people.'

It is always difficult to implement any action from arm's length; to expect results as well is asking a lot. The fact that these overseas Chinese are seen as Chinese does no service to the overseas Chinese themselves, as they themselves are not confident in China because of the cultural differences between mainland China and their own home countries. In some cases, sending them to China did no service to their careers.

Time to rock'n'roll

Foster's was already an established international brand, a solid product of consistent quality, when it sought to enter the Chinese market. This meant it was a product with the potential to be accepted easily by consumers and the company had great confidence. Foster's believed that Chinese consumers would flock to buy its beer, as much as could be produced.

With a population of 1.3 billion, one bottle per person was all that was needed, it was reasoned. Foster's was certainly not the only company that had this attitude about the Chinese market, only to find out later that the formula is not so simple. Sales projections showed this was realistic and a series of advertising campaigns were launched in three cities.

In Shanghai there was a relaunch of Guangming, the local commodity brand, using the vice-president of production as a figurehead to communicate the message of a local beer at a local price, but with import quality. Theoretically this should be effective and it is still a method used broadly today.

The advertising of the Shanghai brand featured a young Chinese couple drinking beer from champagne glasses with Shanghai's millions of neon lights as a backdrop. This communicated a modern message to the younger generation of Chinese, that beer is the new medium of intimacy. Signage space was also rented at huge cost in the most prominent positions in Shanghai.

In Tianjin, an advertisement including China's 'godfather' of rock'n'roll, Cui Jian, was aired on television. An executive described it thus:

> He was singing in the background, you know in a kind of rebellious tone, in this flashy commercial, 60 seconds on TV. This was really cool for Tianjin at the time, it was like, Wow! What's this? It really got their attention. We pulled off a tremendous campaign, not just on TV, but outdoor and also on radio.

The Tianjin campaign was considered successful by many people. So much so that 40 or 50 trucks lined up outside and the brewery was manufacturing at its peak capacity. In reality, according to Foster's sources, beer was sold at below cost, therefore the greater the sales, the bigger the losses. Reliable figures were not available for research to prove this point as large corporations' financial data is difficult to obtain.

In Guangdong, TV commercials were also used throughout the years of operation and major signage was also leased until 1998, the year before Guangzhou Foster's Brewery was sold. Newspapers were especially used for ceremonial events when VIPs and officials were involved.

All media were used for advertising in Shanghai, Guangzhou and Tianjin, including TV, radio, newspapers, posters and signage. In Shanghai, magazines were also used to advertise Shanghai Foster's Brewery. Magazine, newspaper, poster and radio ads carried a strong message of joint venture and management personnel being Australian.

This approach was clearly to show that Shanghai Foster's Brewery was different from other state-owned enterprises. Australians in the joint venture were used in advertisements to convince the public, and 'Sino-Australian joint venture' (中澳合资) was clearly visible on all packaging materials.

Tianjin was the only city where major road signage was not used because it appeared not to be cost effective. Because none of the plants reached a break-even point, it is difficult to determine which medium of advertising was more effective. Moreover, the effectiveness of each medium was not accurately assessed, and from time to time questions were raised about whether certain advertising was necessary, especially when costs were looked at. A typical comment was:

> We did television advertising in China, why? Distribution builds brands and if a consumer sees your advertising on television and then can't find your product anywhere, then you've wasted your money. More than that, they sort of say 'It can't be a very successful product because I liked the ads but I don't see it anywhere'.

Signage proved to be a costly exercise for Foster's. Although generally ineffective, it is a widely used method of advertising in China.

Consumer perceptions of Australia

An early problem for Foster's was choosing advertising agencies. There were no suitable agencies with Western advertising expertise and an understanding of Chinese culture. In the early 1990s there were few advertising agencies in China and agencies from Hong Kong have been used in more recent years, as has ACNielsen.

The extremely strong position of Foster's in Australia gave the company a false perception of its brand awareness and position in the context of the international market. Foster's put itself in the same group as other international brands such as McDonald's, Coca-Cola, Heineken, etc. But it was questionable whether Foster's, as a brand, had the same level of awareness in China as those.

To many Chinese consumers, Australia is a small country with small consumer brands, and Foster's was unknown. Even adding a kangaroo to the label apparently did not create a connection in consumers' minds between the beer and Australia. For many Chinese, brewing is a concept associated with European culture, not the Australian Outback. Foster's later changed TV commercials to focus on a message of Australian lifestyle: the beach, the Outback and relaxed living.

The strong positioning of Foster's as Australian did not allow for creativity in advertising from its head office, over and above the Australian aspect, to bring brand relevance to Chinese consumers. When Heineken launched Reeb (beer spelt backwards), Foster's launched Regal (lager spelt backwards). Foster's Lager as a brand had to add the word beer simply because the word lager had no connection to beer in the mind of many Chinese consumers.

The Shanghai Dragon Girl advertisement was the most controversial. It was created by George Patterson of Melbourne and aimed to capture the European market. The full-body tattoo on the girl could be perceived as a symbol of the 1930s gangster culture of Shanghai and was a mix of perceptions of Shanghai and Chinese culture from a Westerner's point of view.

As an advertisement for Shanghai Beer, it was successful only in London. But from the time it was developed, all personnel in the Chinese sales and marketing team used it. The advertisement indicated the lack of understanding by Australians of Chinese culture and highlights yet again what research for this book found: lack of cultural understanding affects the success of an Australian operation in China, and just how wide the gap is between the two cultures.

Some of the younger members of the marketing team were interested in using this advertisement in most recent years. The Shanghai Dragon Girl advertisement was observed recently in the Shanghai Long Bar, a popular destination for expatriates in Shanghai, and owned by a Westerner. Shanghai Dragon Girl is still culturally unsuited for Chinese consumers because it represents an Orientalist image that is designed to appeal to Westerners.

Personal selling and other sales techniques

Personal selling was used by Foster's in Shanghai for only a very short time and was based on the simple, old-fashioned door-to-door sales technique. The sales and marketing manager for China between 1994 and 1996 came through the Melbourne brewery and had many years of experience. In China he conducted many training programs for local sales people and is believed to be the only person to walk around the market and talk to distributors. He achieved good results and extended the customer list.

The reason other sales and marketing people, regardless of their nationalities, had not used such a simple sales technique could be because of their background and training; the others did not have a background in sales. Most had majored in marketing, some with a Master's degree, so they were equipped with marketing theories and practices. Sales was not one of their strengths.

A large number of sales promotions were carried out constantly in all three cities. Price discounting and tasting promotions were the most common methods. The biggest sales promotion was the official launch of the Foster's brand in China, in Guangzhou in June 1995. It was, in effect, the launch of the first batch of Chinese-brewed Foster's Lager, and it was described by the chief operating officer of Foster's China at the time as a 'significant milestone in the implementation of Foster's China strategy'. Although it was suggested at the time that the launch was too early, the timing was considered critical to keep ahead of other international brands.

The launch of Largo in Tianjin was an expensive exercise but was considered to be successful. It was a new Foster's brand aimed at supplying local consumers with a local product, brewed using Chinese techniques and using rice instead of barley. Largo was sold at a local price and was a product of a strategy to marry consistent quality with local standards and price. The use of rice makes the brewing process slightly different from using barley, which is normally turned into malt first, either by the brewery or purchased.

In Shanghai there were many launches for several brands. At the start of the joint venture launch of Shanghai Beer, the existing brand of the Chinese partner (and still a strong brand today) had to be put on hold for six months. It was a difficult situation in which the brand was being 'farmed out' by the Ministry of Light Industry at various times to help smaller breweries to survive.

Because many smaller breweries were producing the Shanghai brand elsewhere, the quality was inconsistent and uncontrollable. It was unclear how many of these types of contracts had been signed or were operating. The decision to delay was in order to clear all existing stock from the market; it had a shelf life of six months but, as mentioned, use-by dates were not always followed.

The first relaunch, with new packaging and labelling, was in 1994. The promotional theme emphasised the joint venture and Australian management. Promotions were scheduled every three months and customers were rewarded with small gifts, such as key rings, umbrellas, etc.

Employing young women for promotion campaigns, although politically incorrect, was a common strategy also used by other international breweries. Young women were sent to restaurants, shopping centres and department stores. Some restaurants organised different brands for promotion on different nights and there were times when five or six brands were competing at the one promotion site. Obviously, the Australian managers did not like this but continued to take part in these promotions because other brands were doing the same thing.

A lesson in cultural behaviour

The launch of Eazy in Guangdong advertised that every two crown seals handed in entitled a customer to one free beer. Neither Australians nor overseas Chinese had considered that false crown seals might be produced for profiteering. A former manager recalls: 'Normally in Australia you get about 20–30 per cent of people sending something back. We got more than 100 per cent return and soon realised that our distributor was printing them.'

A major cross-cultural difficulty is the inability to comprehend the other's behaviour. Culture is influenced by the environment, historical factors, the political system and many other internal and external factors. The Chinese had been through the Cultural Revolution and 50 years of a socialist system. Improving their income level was a far stronger urge for most Chinese than for Australians, few of whom are brought up lacking basic necessities.

The crown seals fraud was a case in point. As a marketing strategy, Foster's decided to put crown seals inside caps as a reward. Australian marketers were warned but did not believe anyone would open all the caps to search for crowns, without drinking the beer. But the shop owners did indeed open all the stock, then re-capped the bottles. Instead of giving the reward to the customers, the shop owners collected all the extra stock to improve their profit margin.

Foster's has performed well in all other parts of the world in selling its products. One of its major strategies is corporate communication. One of Australian's biggest sporting events became the Foster's Melbourne Cup in 1985. Foster's has been the major sponsor of several leading sports events with a worldwide focus, such as Formula One motor racing and ASP Men's Championship surfing. In 2004 Shanghai hosted its first Formula One race and brand awareness gained from the Foster's presence at the event has been huge.

The price structure in Australia meant that one standard drink cost roughly 0.0017 per cent of average monthly income. In China, a drink of premium beer cost 0.14 per cent of average monthly income. Even at the lower end of the commodity range, a standard drink still represented 0.004 per cent. That is still more than twice as much as in Australia, so premium brand prices would have been impossible for most Chinese to afford. In terms of volume, China was certainly very attractive to marketers. However, the situation has changed much since then. China as a market today provides international brands with high-volume as well as high-income consumers.

Cultural differences are the biggest of many challenges for international firms marketing their products in China. Without an understanding of these differences, marketers are unable to comprehend consumer behaviour and may adopt inappropriate strategies. Over-confidence or an arrogant attitude based on previous success can lead to total failure in a new national market.

Marketers should not take market information and distribution channels for granted. Cultural differences in China have to be analysed, fully understood and then accepted and dealt with, using the right strategies to ensure that products will reach customers. Thorough research before entering a new market is crucial to any strategy and only when all the marketing dynamics are considered and acted on will an organisation compete successfully in a cross-cultural international market.

Since its open-door policy shift in 1979, China has made great and rapid progress. Economically, it has changed from a totally centrally planned economy into a mix of centrally planned plus a market economy. This makes China a very complex market. In addition, it has been shown that Chinese consumers have low tolerance towards unadaptable marketing approaches because of their culture and economic structure. Too many organisations have failed in China because they have had an inflexible approach.

This chapter is based mainly on the Foster's experience and is merely a sample of how one organisation among many has failed when not taking cultural differences into account to the extent necessary for success.

References

De Long, David, and Fahey, Liam, 2000, Diagnosing cultural barriers to knowledge management, *Academy of Management Executive*, 14(4), 113.

Ehrman, Chaim Meyer, and Hamburg, Morris, 1986, Information search for foreign direct investment using two-stage country selection procedures: A new procedure, *Journal of International Business Studies*, 17(2), 93–116.

Frewen, Stephen R., and Mosely, Stephen C., 1995, Coping with distribution in China, *The Economist Conferences Executive Forums*, Beijing, China.

Kotler, P., Armstrong, G., Brown, L., and Adam, S., 1998, *Marketing* (4th ed.) (New York/Sydney: Prentice Hall).

Purves, Bill, 1991, *Barefoot in the Boardroom – Venture and Misadventure in the People's Republic of China* (Sydney: Allen & Unwin).

Shanghai Foster's Brewery, 1993, *Feasibility Study* (Foster's Brewing Limited, Melbourne).

11

Conclusion

Since China's open-door policy began in 1978, Western companies have been trying to do business there. It may seem ironic after nearly 35 years, a book title: 'Doing Business Successfully in China' is still needed. The key word here is 'successfully'.

In reality, many companies have got it wrong in China and they are still getting it wrong. This is alarming because there is no shortage of publications advising business people what they should do, but when it comes to putting words into practice, Westerners simply do not get it.

This raises two key questions: what is the problem and what is the solution? The answer to both is bicultural personnel.

China is a unique market-place in the world. To start with, it is a socialist system with special characteristics. It is a centrally planned economy but has the characteristics of market economy. Western organisations only have experience of operating in a market economy. This fundamental gap can only be addressed by bridging through understanding from both sides. Any attempt to fix the problem with a one sided effort has not worked and will not work.

The concept of this book was to illustrate how business is done in China and to stress the fundamental message that the key to success is the engagement of bicultural personnel.

On finishing the book I am seeing a company making the same mistakes and on the verge of losing a project of $320 million, a golden opportunity, and perhaps an opportunity of the century in China, and it might well be the last very exciting one of its kind in China.

The evolution of investment opportunities in China

Business and investment opportunities in China today are very different from 30 years ago. China now has the world's largest foreign currency reserves and is cash-ready for acquisitions, mergers and investments overseas and at home. China no longer needs the foreign direct investment that it required previously. The Chinese Government is tightening its investment policies to protect its national interests. There is a growing trend and support among Chinese to protect the country's national interests, identity and resources.

The changes made towards this were first seen in 2001 (?) to the joint venture law. In the more recent years there has been a drive by the government to buy back shares from joint ventures. At the same time, the Government is imposing limitations and regulations on new ventures to discouraging those that are not in the national interest.

There may well be a change in the near future to foreign direct investments not being encouraged. Already the minimum investment level was lifted in the last update of the joint venture law.

From the investors' side, there have been degrees of changes on the purpose of investments. In the 1980s and 1990s, Western companies were aiming for economies of scale, cheap labour and cheap resources. Although most of them are still leveraging on the cheap labour aspect, companies have since put more focus on China's 1.33 billion consumers. Therefore, it is even more important for Western companies to pay a great deal of attention to Chinese culture and cultural differences.

China: a costly laboratory

China has been a large, costly laboratory for many multinational companies over the past 30 years. The disappointing part is that not many organisations have learnt much from either their own mistakes or someone else's.

Foreign companies are still prone to arrogance about their business models many of which would embarrass the 16-century Portuguese traders. As recently as March 2011, Martell had to close its flagship store in Shanghai. Best Buy and DIY group, both US retail chains, were forced to close their stores because they refused to acknowledge that Chinese consumers are culturally different from those from America. They also failed to adopt models that are effective for the Chinese market.

Why are companies still ignoring advice or are not able to take advice?

Fundamentally, the answer is culturally driven.

As humans we are programmed in a system we are brought up with. We act consciously and unconsciously according to these codes. At times we are unable to break out of them and behave differently because these cultural restrictions are built into us like a blue-print for our thoughts and actions. According to Charles Darwin, this is so we are able to adapt into the environment we live in and survive in it. Hence, changing the blue- print cannot be a quick exercise. For some people it may require a lifetime of practice or in most cases generations. However, according to Cultural Capability

Theory, this is also achievable in a shorter time by other individuals.

China is a complex market with multiple sub-markets. There must be hundreds of stories written by now on failures and successes in China (sadly, there is more failure than success). Some organisations took no notice of any advice. Some blindly followed generic advice without looking at their own situation. Just like when a new baby is born. Everyone gives advice on how to raise him or her, and the advice is valuable, but every baby is different.

Cultural issues are generally intangible and invisible, which is the reason they are ignored or overseen. However, when they become visible it is usually because they are at a stage that it has gone too far and too deep. It is similar to of health issues; early symptoms of a heart attack are often over-looked until it occurs. Sometimes it is too late.

If we understand the concept of not having too much salt in our diet to prevent a heart attack then we would also understand the advice on avoiding the negative cultural costs in doing business with China to avoid fatal failures.

Doing business successfully in China

To be successful in China starts with a culturally sound strategy. A strategy that is not culturally suited is like building a house with a leaking roof. Constant repairing is required therefore it will always end up costing more.

A culturally suited strategy means looking at the Chinese market (preferably one specific part, not all of it), and taking into consideration a whole range of matters: its political and economic structure; the real role and power of government and the party; the legal system and its practice; the business culture and its relationship-based practices; the concept of guanxi and the value of 'face', understanding insider and outside concepts; and of course the special cultural characteristics of consumers.

There are several challenges in achieving these objectives. To start with, understanding each of these concepts is not simple. Even when you have comprehended, the way to grasp and practice them presents another bigger challenge. Then, consistently applying the acquired knowledge on all occasions is another challenge. Furthermore when each new scenario emerges, it may be different from the previous experience, because culture is dynamic.

The unique Chinese political structure is one of the most difficult elements of doing business with China. Efforts by Chinese government and organisations to make the system and process transparent at the request and urging by Western organisations, does not necessarily help with the end result. This is because their effort of trying to make something that is completely different into something that everyone is familiar with, simply does not translate. In a simple analogy, to try to make a dragon look like a tiger will not work if people only know what a tiger looks like, but not a dragon.

The argument here that is that it is better for organisations to recognise the nature of China and doing business with it, and from that starting point they will be better at learning how to deal with the beast to achieve their objectives.

The Chinese Government is governed by the Chinese Communist Party, which has unique autonomy and control over the country's economic system. For example, when the real estate market heated up to what was considered as a danger level, the Government was able to legislate early in 2011 this year to limit couples to buying and owning two properties. In a pure market economy, this type of interference would have not been possible.

I highlight the role of government and the party because they, in turn have an impact on the legal system and its practice.

To learn and master these Chinese differences is not easy for those not emersed in the environment and culture. The speed of development in China has been such that what has been achieved in 30 years is equal to the accomplishments by the West in 150 years, through a process of learning that has been slow and time consuming.

It is too slow for modern-day China and organisations may find themselves falling behind their competitors. Organisations must fast track their processes where possible and the answer to that is bicultural personnel.

These are the people who understand, operate and communicate in both cultures naturally and comfortably. They are the key to opening the large and heavy red gates of China. Bicultural personnel are the competitive advantage that organisations must have along the path to success.

Index

Printed and bound by CPI Group (UK) Ltd, Croydon, CR0 4YY

08/05/2025

01864969-0001